D1366562

Individuals from Vastly Different Political Perspectives Agree That There Is a Crisis in Education

CRISIS
IN THE
CLASSROOM
CRISIS IN EDUCATION

DR. BENJAMIN CARSON

BENJAMIN CRUMP, ESQ.

ARMSTRONG WILLIAMS

Skyhorse Publishing

Skyhorse Publishing books may be purchased in bulk at special discounts for sales promotion, corporate gifts, fund-raising, or educational purposes. Special editions can also be created to specifications. For details, contact the Special Sales Department, Skyhorse Publishing, 307 West 36th Street, 11th Floor, New York, NY 10018 or info@skyhorsepublishing.com.

Skyhorse® and Skyhorse Publishing® are registered trademarks of Skyhorse Publishing, Inc.®, a Delaware corporation.

Visit our website at www.skyhorsepublishing.com.

10 9 8 7 6 5 4 3 2 1

Library of Congress Cataloging-in-Publication Data is available on file.

Hardcover ISBN: 978-1-5107-7688-3
Ebook ISBN: 978-1-5107-7689-0

Cover design by Brendan Nieto

Printed in the United States of America

CONTENTS

2016: Benjamin Crump, Esq. (left), Dr. Benjamin Carson (center), and Armstrong Williams (right) celebrating the 90th birthday of Williams' mother, Thelma Williams, on his family's South Carolina farm.

A PRELUDE TO THE CRISIS

---

by Armstrong Williams

H. G. Welles famously noted that "Civilization is a race between education and catastrophe."

President George Washington's first State of the Union Address underscored the nexus between education and constitutional governance celebrating liberty and the rule of law:

> Knowledge is in every Country the surest basis of public happiness. In one, in which the measures of Government receive their impression so immediately from the sense of the Community as in ours, it is proportionably essential. To the security of a free Constitution it contributes in various ways: By convincing those, who are entrusted with the public administration, that every valuable end of Government is best

answered by the enlightened confidence of the people: And by teaching the people themselves to know and to value their own rights; to discern and provide against invasions of them; to distinguish between oppression and the necessary exercise of lawful authority; between burthens proceeding from a disregard to their convenience and those resulting from the inevitable exigencies of Society; to discriminate the spirit of liberty from that of licentiousness, cherishing the first, avoiding the last, and uniting a speedy, but temperate vigilance against encroachments, with an inviolable respect to the laws.

In our postindustrial society, brains, not brawn, command the highest compensation and rewards. And, in the digital age, effortless access to all the greatest books and learning in the world, including a free de facto college education, are available to all who are willing to study in lieu of squandering time on juvenile amusements.

Yet education is in a free fall in the United States despite climbing per pupil expenditures. Each year, the collective IQ or knowledge of leaders and the citizenry plunges to new depths of ignorance. Even members of Congress are clueless about the three branches of government and the allocation of constitutional responsibilities. Students know virtually nothing about history—even of Watergate or the Vietnam War. The alphabet has not escaped extinction as emojis displace literary masterpieces, such as, "We hold these truths to be self-evident, that all Men are created equal, that they are endowed by their Creator with certain unalienable rights, that among these are life, liberty, and the pursuit of happiness."

What explains the paradox of our epidemic of illiteracy and the riches of instantly available wisdom and learning, like Samuel Taylor Coleridge's "Water, water everywhere, nor any drop to drink," from the *Rime of the Ancient Mariner?*

The blame lies in the indolence and indifference of educators, parents, and students alike. It is said that genius is 99 percent perspiration and 1 percent inspiration, but such efforts will not be forthcoming without motivation. That requires honoring debating talents and intellectual achievements above the hormonal amusements or titillations of sports, singing, dancing, or modeling. The Kim Kardashians and Justin Biebers of the world should be ostracized for trivializing life, not aped or parroted.

Plutarch's *Life of Pericles* explains: "Therefore it was a fine saying of Antisthenes, when he heard that Ismenias was an excellent piper: 'But he's a worthless man' said he, 'otherwise he wouldn't be so good a piper.' And so Philip once said to his son, who, as the wine went round, plucked the strings charmingly and skillfully, 'Art not ashamed to pluck the strings so well?'"

Students can be excused for their misplaced priorities. We are all born 99.9 percent hormonal and 0.1 percent reflective. Maturation is the process of reversing those percentages.

Educators and parents have no excuse. The former is guilty of educational malpractice in graduating students unable to read or write proficiently, and the latter is guilty of parental malpractice by giving birth to children they are unwilling to instruct and inspire in the search for truth without ulterior motives. Parents are morally obligated to read to their children, for example, *Uncle Tom's Cabin*, *Don Quixote*, Greek Mythology, or Frederick Douglass's *The Heroic Slave*, and to fill the house with literature, newspapers, and magazines. Television, movies, and radio should generally be banned as toxins to the mind.

Every year, thousands of children who will never be taxpayers in society and never enter the workforce are sent out into the world incapable of independent living. These kids are slaves to their hormonal cravings. They inevitably become wards of the state without the pride of accomplishment. They have neither hopes nor dreams.

Baltimore public schools are emblematic of dysfunctional education. Political leaders fiddle while education crumbles. The price of such irresponsibility is steep. It produces inmates rather than taxpayers. Homeless persons rather than homeowners. Crime-infested streets rather than parks dotted with daisies and tulips. Drug rehabilitation centers in lieu of baseball diamonds and basketball courts. And guns rather than books.

Politicians do not care because teachers, parents, and

students do not care. Have you ever heard of a popular protest for omitting from the curriculum Aristotle, Plato, Aristophanes, Marcus Aurelius, Plutarch, Maimonides, Thomas Aquinas, Shakespeare, John Milton, Victor Hugo, ad infinitum? The protests are over educational sub-trivialities.

Family is a significant culprit. Single motherhood and adolescent pregnancy rates in minority communities during the previous century have produced generations of children without a second parent, who were born into poverty and lacked nutrition and adequate habitation. They are born burdened with figurative chains in the race of life.

Politicians leave welfare undisturbed to attract the votes of their government dependents, while welfare recipients leave politicians undisturbed to maintain or hike their unearned government benefits. It is a form of pathological domestic abuse in which the wife returns to her abuser out of necessity.

From the founding of the United States, government and politicians used Blacks for personal and financial gains from working the fields to building infrastructure, to experimentation by the medical industry. The medical industry used Blacks for experimentation that often led to lifelong ailments or death. The government has been the worst enemy of Blacks. The Civil Rights Act and Voting Rights Act and the Civil War Amendments are the exceptions to the rule. What the government gives with one hand, it takes away with the other. One step forward. One step back. Promises are broken as regularly as the rising and setting of the sun. Fool me once, shame on you. Fool me twice, shame on me.

The crisis has impacted families in ways unimaginable, but their stories are real and riveting of the incumbent problems in urban cities across the United States. Reviewing Project Baltimore's efforts to combat school failures over the last five years reveals that every parent interviewed had a child who is either a victim of the education system or is dead. That's right, dead.

Sadly, even when conversing with those parents, the terrible cycle of victimization by the Baltimore City school district continues to show its ugly face, indicating that they, too, were victims of that same school system. These men and women are at least thirty years old and their victimization by the school system is evident by their inability to communicate, their inability to read, and their inability to write; they tremble at every word, working ten times as hard to conjure what comes off their tongues. You can see the embarrassment of inarticulateness.

It is a devastating blow to the human spirit and listening to these parents you also see their dreams for a better future for their children. You clearly see that they know they were cheated, but pray and hope that those same failures that robbed them of a future do not consume their own children. But the harsh reality is that it typically does. This is perhaps one of the greatest robberies in the United States, and if it were a financial crime or any other crime for that matter, dozens would be charged, prosecuted, and likely face jail time, but that is not the case here, and we must ask why. We must ask why this is acceptable when people are being robbed of an opportunity to make a good life. Are we all so selfishly absorbed by our own daily problems that we're complacent with the grand larceny of our children's futures?

The children who attend dilapidated schools are survivors of a corrupt system that frankly does not care about them. To politicians, they are nothing but votes, and for education administrators they are expendables. These communities are populated by the unschooled. Why? Because the educated leave; they move out of the city to enable their children to escape from the debilitating maleducation they experienced. But more stay behind with neither hope nor ambition.

CRISIS
IN THE
CLASSROOM

2015: Williams and Carson take a lighthearted break from Williams' SIRIUS XM RADIO broadcast program in Washington, DC.

2017: Crump with Williams at South Carolina State University with former South Carolina State University President James Clarke as Williams donates $250,000 to the University.

ESSAYS BY
ARMSTRONG WILLIAMS

THE CRISIS OF DISSENT

Our inner cities have been plagued by violence, fueled by political actors who care more about power than people. Their malfeasance and nonfeasance regarding public health and safety have caused our inner cities to erode and crumble beneath our feet, begetting desolate wastelands rife with violence and crime with appalling murder rates. Parents keep their children in at night. The elderly do not dare sit on the porch. Even the police are daunted from entering "no-go" areas. They incubate crime. The innocent are preyed upon.

Having children is a huge responsibility; one ought to be conscious of bringing children into the world without the commitment to embrace a moral compass and to raise them, because if not, they will prey on other children, sucking many of them into a life of crime and violence perpetrated against hardworking innocent people of their own communities. In some cases, a child's future is written at birth. Imagine that: You are born, and you are not given a choice; the road has already been paved for you merely because of your environment. If it were me, I would be angry and disappointed at widespread complacency or condonation of injustice with impunity. Wouldn't you feel the same?

Many children die before they have had a chance to live. I recall one sad story in Washington, D.C., the nation's capital, and the place I call home. During one of many violent weekends, multiple youths were murdered, including a fifteen- and eighteen-year-old—their God-given talents never had a chance to flower and flourish.

Minority communities encourage dangerous subcultures that elevate violence and drugs that are often glorified in rap music. Young minority men are captured only to die or be imprisoned for a hormonal race to self-destruction. Music should inspire us to follow the better angels of our nature, not lure us into the depths of depravity unsuited for manhood.

Men defend the home and the community. They are role models. Without them, gangs and crime flourish. Young males plunge into violence, crime, and sexual promiscuity. The secret of crime fighting is good fathers who insist on discipline and learning with no excuses.

Do not forget the collateral damage of the crime epidemic in the inner cities: innocent kids murdered while going to and from school or playing at the park in cities like Chicago. They are the rule, not the exception. Criminals are remorseless and prey on the good and the bad without discrimination. There is no light at the end of the tunnel.

Imagine being terrified by walking to your car or jogging

in your neighborhood, fearful of gun violence. Parents naturally worry about their children being out of sight but imagine worrying about your child within walking distance. That is the reality for many urban families who are powerless to diminish the danger. They do not deserve that, nobody does. Political leaders are MIA. Police are handicapped. Children are targeted by gang members. At the root of so much of this pain and carnage is education.

I once spoke to a student from Madison, Wisconsin about how failing educational systems lead to rising crime. He said that the dropout rates among teenagers in schools are so high that it ought to be considered a modern-day civil rights issue, that it affects primarily Black and brown kids who are poor, leaving them unable to survive and make a living. In other words, "they turn to the streets because it is the only other option they have." My conversation with him reminded me of just how fragile our young people are and how easy and fast it is to lose them to outside forces without structure and education. Like Dr. Jekyll and Mr. Hyde, they segue from victims to victimizers. The plunge is normalized and escapes ostracism.

The crimes warrant national attention to secure safe conditions for all. If nothing is done, crime will continue to sound the death knell for minority inner-city communities. Education is the obvious answer to crime and poverty. But formidable forces defend the status quo.

Our policymakers must be strong-armed into doing what

is right, which will both lead to a better tomorrow and quench the policymaker's thirst for power. Change never happens by spontaneous combustion. The status quo always has fierce defenders. Communities of color can no longer be a cesspool for violence, drugs, and prostitution. Communities should be safe havens for residents spawning the next generations of entrepreneurs, innovators and inventors, educators, doctors, lawyers, and so many other professions. But they are not in most inner cities across the United States. Indeed, they beget violence and violent criminals who rule the roost.

Political demagogues exploit public gullibility to divert attention from genuine ills by concocting differences where unity is imperative. Contrary to orthodoxy, race plays no role in our failing education systems. There is one color that governments and school administrators care about—as one guest on a town hall I hosted said, "It ain't about the color of your skin, it is about the color of your money."

Attaching race, religion, sex, sexual orientation, and the plethora of other things that make us different from one another is just about the only thing that needs to be stated to convince a broad swath of people from each end of the political spectrum to align their ideals with yours. Yet, despite all that is said about our differences, they are educationally meaningless. Wisdom and knowledge sport no race, religion, or gender.

Speaking truth invites ostracism or vilification, which

encourages silence in the face of falsehoods. Thus, so does ignorance prosper.

This abusive argumentation has become universal, paradoxically finding ostensible defenders of free speech its most vocal adversaries. Whatever happened to Voltaire's reported statement, "I may disapprove of what you say, but I will defend to the death your right to say it"?

When the government speaks, it speaks volumes—people listen. Whether one believes the government is trustworthy, it possesses the resources to brainwash. When the government speaks nonsense, people adopt that nonsense as their own and use collective action to harm our communities. It is the same with politicians, not-for-profit organizations, and other political advocacy groups. They are ventriloquists and we are their dummies.

During a Crisis in the Classroom town hall of mine, a woman discussed first-hand accounts of individual teachers kowtowing to the pressures of school administrators who intimidated them and threatened their careers if they went public about the inefficiencies and issues within the school systems where they were employed.

Due to the harsh consequences of deviating from the widespread perception of what is right and what is wrong, up-and-coming politicians and lone wolves vying to make a positive change in the world are too afraid to speak up. They are practically silenced before they can make a difference. As a result, our minority communities have borne the brunt of poorly conceived but popular policies that benefit the makers but not the purported beneficiaries.

Murder rates, burglaries, sexual assault, gang violence, and petty theft are all skyrocketing because of the government silencing truth-telling. Today, it is more favorable for candidates and politicians to make vague, open-ended promises about what they will do to help minority communities instead of working towards solutions. Convincing people in minority communities that they need to get an education and that they must work to be their best selves and fulfill their responsibilities in their role as good citizens is unpopular, a far cry from *Invictus*, "I am the master of my fate. I am the captain of my soul."

I have traveled the country and visited some of the worst school systems in the United States. I have seen how politicians failed the communities and how they have utilized their power to silence those who would likely make a difference.

When people are in despair, those in power gain by exploiting hope with promises as worthless as a munificent bequest in a pauper's will. Politicians do not want to solve problems; they want them to fester to give them campaign issues to rally their troops. To them, a solution is a catastrophe.

In 2022, despite all the failings of the Baltimore County School district, the Baltimore County School Board unanimously approved a $50 million supplemental budget to fund staff raises over the next several years. This raise was justified to further the interests of the children. The school district has a budget of over $2 billion and generally ranks among the highest school districts in per-pupil expenditures despite dismal student performances.

Minority communities fall victim to the divisive rhetoric of politicians; they pit themselves against members of their community and believe that they must be divided because they are different. They use the talking points and ideals of figureheads to speak down to their minority brothers and sisters who dare to think differently. This government speech not only harms their interests, but it divides them. Those in minority communities must be steadfast and see through the bad actors who seek to do them harm. They must ask themselves questions, not simply look for answers.

If one wanders into an inner city today, one encounters dilapidated homes, sketchy figures, and a breeding ground of terror that evokes a desire to flee. The destitution forces minority communities into a corner with nowhere to go. On the one hand, they may not see the fruits of a thriving economy as no outsiders enter to spend money and create jobs and other opportunities, and no insiders are equipped to replace the outsiders. When this happens, which is customary, developers roll in and make offers that destitute families cannot refuse. They force them out of their neighborhoods and cram them into high-density areas, leaving them worse off than they were before. Worse yet, because home ownership is so low among minority communities, it is not even as if many of these minority families are provided with an influx of cash to give them opportunities elsewhere. Instead, their landlords are bought out, their rent is jacked up, and they are forced out of the community—communities in which they may have lived for generations. That is the ugly face of gentrification.

But of course, no one is stopping this. No one is stopping minorities from leaving their roots and moving elsewhere. Instead, powerful interests, using false facts and cleverly crafted racial arguments, can silence any dissenting voices and allow for the continuation and proliferation of a community's end.

The media is complicit. They arbitrate truth and silence dissent. Our First Amendment prohibits the government from making laws that infringe on our right to speech, yet they do not prohibit the government from speaking. With its power to speak, the government can whisper in the ears of the mainstream media out of the view of the public and provide them with false or misleading facts and inferences that they can then parrot to the public to control what they think. The media is compensated greatly for their services by being the recipient of leaks and front-page breaking news stories that win journalism awards.

Even when the government screws up, it can conceal failures with its private partners. When a story breaks, the government can go to their friends in the media and mislead the public or bury the story. The government can feed only the good and not the bad to the powerful interest groups who propagate their ideas.

The lengths that the media goes to cover their tracks and paint the opposition as the enemy is boundless, going so far as to write off the promotion of racial division in schools as a conspiracy theory. During one Crisis in the Classroom town hall, I was told by a guest of her experience with a school district in Evanston, Illinois that was taking teachers through training telling them that they were evil because of their race.

Flipping through the pages of any newspaper, it is easy to see what the result has been of decades-long collusion between government actors and media actors. The news section has been invaded by the opinion section and people are fed conclusions instead of facts. No longer are people afforded the opportunity to undertake their own research based on what they read to determine what the truth is. Instead, they are spoon-fed what the media and government want them to believe.

Worse, the media frequently has the problems spoon-fed to them too, but regularly fails to report on them—seemingly for political or other business-related reasons. The leader of Project Baltimore informed me, during a Crisis in the Classroom segment, that internal literacy testing in the Baltimore City schools found that 77 percent of high school students read at only an elementary school level. And even worse, these internal reports were not publicized by the school—instead, they were only uncovered when a distraught teacher leaked these reports to Project Baltimore. Yet, this devastating news hardly moved mountains, in fact, it hardly made a difference at all. It was just another unfortunate fact that died as soon as it came to light.

Since we are only told of what is wrong instead of being told all the facts that have led up to the thing being wrong, we are forced to come up with solutions that might make things worse rather than being able to address the source of the problem. We must scramble to do what is right, ultimately failing in the process because the truth was hidden from us. Because we aren't given the facts, people and politicians will invariably create their own reasons for the failure and will fight tooth and nail until their solutions are accepted as authoritative.

These arguments unfortunately tend to plunge to the least common denominator, that is the discrimination perceived as the source of all evil. Even though the solution might have been clear had we then known the facts and not merely the solutions, we might have been able to determine what was wrong before falsehoods proliferated. Now, the people will be forced to contend with that which is unobjectionable along with the string of coincidentally similar arguments that are cobbled together to create a broader one—that the issue is one of our differences and not of something else.

Minority political leaders have unfortunately failed

minority communities in the same ways as their non-minority counterparts. They have focused so much on matters of race while ignoring the very real plight that minorities confront that is unrelated to race. In America, we sink or swim together. Strong families with a strong sense of community, individual pride, access to a good education, and access to opportunities are like Archimedes' lever: "If you give me a lever and a good place to stand, I can move the world."

I reflect on the Baltimore public school system, which has failed minority kids for years, and not a single politician has been awakened from slumber. Students are graduating from high school reading at third-grade levels. Basic math is beyond their ken. Students progress to the next grade level notwithstanding failing grades. No outrage. Graduation into a life of violence is inescapable. They have no skills for any other trade. We will be condemned by history for letting it happen.

The future is what each of us individually makes it, but what does it cost us as a society if we do nothing to help motivate our fellow Americans to rise to their full potential? Every child is born with freedom in this country, but are they truly free if they are born in an environment that robs them of freedom before they even have a chance? I do not think so, which is why minority Americans must hold their political leaders accountable and look internally at the cultural changes the community needs to make in order to prosper. But the need has wider application. All Americans should come together to make everyone succeed in their ambitions because a rising tide lifts all boats. Politics is not about winning or losing. It is about making everyone a winner and giving everyone a helping hand when necessitated by the vicissitudes of life.

In the end, it seems that those who purport to unify us are indeed dividing us. Minority communities can be made safer and minority people can thrive if they are unafraid to speak up about the conditions of their communities and if they are given the facts and opportunities to think of creative solutions, address problems that directly cause their suffering, and hold those accountable who put them down.

THE CRISIS OF TRANSPARENCY

The first thing you learn about the government at the macro level is a fetish for secrecy to conceal blunders, crimes, and mismanagement. The Baltimore City school system is emblematic. As Justice Louis D. Brandeis instructed, "Sunshine is said to be the best of disinfectants; the electric lamp the most efficient policeman."

The government weaponizes secrecy to deceive and brainwash the public. Character assassination is employed to discredit truth-tellers.

Transparency is one of, if not the key marker of a healthy nation. How can you have government by the consent of the governed without knowing what the government is doing? Attaining power is difficult, but some will go to great lengths to attain and retain it, including concealment of wrongdoing or stupidity.

We would be better off if the government were honest about missteps and upfront about everything that is occurring inside the government. That would equip us with the knowledge necessary to root out evil and solve issues. But lies are easier and typically more lucrative.

A teacher reported to Project Baltimore that she was instructed to manipulate test scores to graduate students. When Project Baltimore received this information, they conducted an urgent investigation and, upon discovering more evidence of grade fixing, notified the Baltimore City school system. They were informed that the Baltimore City school system would investigate.

After more than a year, the Baltimore City school system released a report and published a statement claiming that Project Baltimore's claims were unfounded. Project Baltimore filed a Freedom of Information Act request to get the study purporting to demonstrate that Project Baltimore's allegations were unfounded. After a lengthy battle, the Baltimore City School District ultimately issued the study.

The released study consisted of 12,000 pages of black-lined, redacted material, which effectively covered the whole report.

Project Baltimore immediately filed a lawsuit to obtain the unredacted report. After a second lawsuit, the Baltimore City District Court ruled in favor of Project Baltimore, compelling the school system to release an unredacted copy of the report, and issuing a scathing opinion admonishing what the Baltimore City school system had done.

The Baltimore City school system then released all the documents that showed mountains of evidence and substantiated claims of grade-fixing, which were uncovered through internal investigations. This seemed to be a complete triumph for Project Baltimore, but subsequent inquiry revealed that the grade manipulation disclosed in the report was just the tip of the iceberg; there was considerably more grade fixing.

Project Baltimore surmises that this is not an isolated case but an epidemic throughout the nation.

Unfortunately, as government actors cause more problems, it is likely that groups like Project Baltimore that strive to expose these reprehensible activities by administrative officials in schools will confront a seemingly insurmountable onslaught of negative press and spurious accusations. With the tidal wave of controversy that invariably engulfs those who oppose powerful groups comes the growing need for more capital and personnel.

Transparency today unfortunately comes at a cost. It is a high price that few can afford and that even fewer are willing to spend the time to fight for. It is increasingly clear that governments and public officials are hiding more than we know just based on their refusal to speak. One would think that a government that professes transparency would be open about the things they do and acknowledge their shortcomings, and so they would at least disclose internal reports that would shed light on internal issues. Unfortunately, as the Project Baltimore lawsuit showed, transparency is paid little mind among government and public officials since transparency can cause them embarrassment, stigma, or even a prison sentence. Ponder the irony of being a publicly funded organization that creates a report paid for by taxpayer dollars and then refuses to disclose that report at every turn.

Power corrupts and a lack of transparency corrupts absolutely irrespective of race or gender. It is in the DNA of the species. The weak suffer the most. Knowledge is their only defense.

If we fail to ensure transparency, then we can be sure that government officials will slither slyly through the shadows and prey upon the weakest figures they can find. Persons from Project Baltimore described the lack of transparency perfectly. They said that when they were informed that many children were having their grades manipulated, they went to the communities to inform them, and they responded that they knew that grade manipulation was occurring on a wide scale. However, because the government lacked transparency and refused to provide hard facts to substantiate what they already knew was true, they were unable to use this fact to rally against the school administrators and effect change.

Without proof, even the most obvious things can be written off as mere conjecture. That is precisely why transparency is so critical. After all, it gives the people the information they need so that they can go against the government, and it directly provides them with evidence of a problem that is based entirely on fact.

It is not merely grade manipulation and similar

reprehensible practices that transparency requires to be made public. It is also the general education of our children. School boards in Maryland and countless more across the country have made it clear that parents are not to be involved in the process of deciding the curriculum that their students will learn or upon the teachers that are hired.

Education is about far more than teaching our perception of right and wrong; it is about allowing our children to decide for themselves what is right and wrong by giving them the critical thinking tools that they need to make that decision. Whether we realize it or not, our morals are heavily influenced by our upbringing. The lessons that our mothers and fathers taught us, the situations that we found ourselves in, and the people that we interacted with all mesh together to create our morality. Thus, when school boards attempt to push parents out of the decision of who teaches them and what they are taught, it takes away the personalized nature of moral discovery and instead creates a uniform structure of morality that forgoes the ideals of one's faith and upbringing.

The South Carolina Commissioner on Education, Terrye Seckinger, told me that "Parents have been boxed out . . . in terms of who is going to lead their schools . . . [and the process of hiring teachers]." By boxing out parents from these decisions, schools become partisan. As I was told by a former educator at a town hall of mine, our education system is and should be bipartisan. This makes sense because we are not sending kids to schools to be Democrats and we are not sending kids to schools to be Republicans. With this simple idea in mind, it should be clear that the only thing that students should learn is how to guide their moral compass. They do not need to be taught that accepting people and not discriminating based on their sexual orientation or the color of their skin is wrong, instead, providing a student with a foundational education should be more than enough to guide them in the right direction—against discrimination and towards acceptance.

But parents are not off the hook. They are most responsible for the morals of their offspring. They teach by example. Parents are thus morally obligated to live impeccable lives of wisdom, courage, generosity, and austerity. They must spend time reading and talking with their children in person and not over the internet or mobile phones. Children of such parents have a better chance to stay away from and navigate drugs and liquor and refrain from overindulging in sexual promiscuity. Their actions will reflect every benevolent instinct of the human heart—taking the nation to the summit of civilization.

The people of the United States and every other country should demand transparency. We need not look further than countries like Russia and China to see how a lack of transparency can oppress people who live under the government's rule, making them willing to accept the word of the government and be fearful of dissenting.

Dissent is a tenet of our nation. Disagreement enables

change, and that change often leads to the betterment of society. However, when the government paints dissenters as the enemy, it simply creates division and causes further regression.

Other than secrecy to protect life, transparency should be the coin of the realm to deter maladministration and wrongdoing. All experience corroborates that precept.

THE CRISIS OF EXPLOITATION

Education is the secret to happiness, comfort, and prosperity. Ignorance is the bedfellow of misery, poverty, and hardship. But education is missing in too many communities. Why? A combination of race and cultural exaltation of juvenile amusements over learning and wisdom.

The weakest are the most vulnerable to exploitation. Minorities are like putty in the hands of politicians and industry—a version of "No minority need apply." Exploitation has no penalties or downsides.

Capital is needed to create more capital. With no resources, minorities find it difficult to gain economic traction. Their influence is diminished in proportion to their inability to make handsome political donations to obtain political access.

The current income disparity between average white and Black households is stark: $75,000 for whites and $45,000 for Blacks. With nearly twice as much money as Blacks and a third more than Hispanics ($55,000), it becomes increasingly clear that minorities have missed out on the opportunities enjoyed by their white counterparts. They have been marginalized in the political arena.

Regressive policies by policymakers and the economic and social abuse of minorities have made them perfect targets for exploitation, cheap labor, and the other plentiful resources they have to offer. Race and impoverishment invite school administrators to exploit minorities for their own gain.

This cycle of poverty has become a generational—a seemingly insurmountable—problem because so many have been lost with no way out. An educator from Maryland, in discussing the faults of the Maryland school systems, told me that during her time as a high school teacher, the administration in her school was asking both her and the faculty to do things that were "criminal." As she stated, "we were asked to pass kids . . . that had not learned . . . a concept, not a skill."

After all, if there is a consistent stream of issues to be solved, and there is a consistent stream of deep-pocketed higher authorities willing to give you money in purporting to solve them, wouldn't you continue to let the problem fester as a profit center? The massive influx of billions upon billions of dollars into failing educational systems has caused administrators to get rich at the expense of those who they were tasked to make succeed.

No archaeological expedition is required to discover

these facts. High school dropout rates are public. Illiteracy rates are public. Crime rates are public. Funding is public. Salaries are public. The biggest controversy of the century is wide out in the open and ready to be told, yet nobody seems to have the courage—or inclination—to tell it.

When good men come to power, they can often be easily corrupted and led astray by the opportunity that lies before them. Money and power can lead any good man down evil paths.

Instead, we require brave men to seek office and do what must be done for the betterment of our communities. Yet, even those who grow up in these communities who grew up seeing the pain and suffering of their neighbors and who rise to power almost invariably do more harm than good. It is easy to blame these people for their misdeeds. But their intentions may be good. The road to hell, however, is paved with good intentions.

Think about it: From a young age, marginalized youth are put into a pipeline that treats the law as against their people. With this idea of inferiority, they easily eat up and regurgitate propaganda from the media and government figures that teach them that their impoverishment is a result of inferiority to a superior race. It gives them excuses and the opportunity to turn those excuses into a justification for indolence and continued failure.

This vicious cycle of wrongful belief in inferiority makes powerful politicians and community leaders merely parrot the ideas of the people who came before them. Those despicable individuals who divided us by race instead of unifying us by our common ancestry under God have had their views recycled and remade into mainstream ideals hidden beneath unobjectionable ones.

The past is a prologue. We are ruled by our past and we will continue to be ruled by it until we end this cycle of abhorrent ideals that serve only those who propagate them.

Throughout my travels both inside and outside the United States, I have witnessed first-hand the effects of malfeasance by school administrators. I have seen the humans, not the statistics, behind failed policies that caused bad education. I have spoken to the children who, despite being in their younger years, are already counting down to their final days, awaiting death by a botched robbery, a stray bullet, a petty dispute, or a gang-style killing.

What I have come to realize throughout my time traveling the United States and seeing those handicapped by a lack of education, is that much deeper strife has been created within people and throughout society. With a climbing number of uneducated paired with nearly boundless methods of earning a living, many have come to believe that education is not necessary for a successful life—that what matters most is one's ability to make money. This has led students who cannot read or write to pursue careers divorced from education.

Many turn to the internet to make a living through jobs

requiring no skills. This is enticing for some, as studies show that there are millions of influencers in the United States—persons whose job it is to entertain others on social media and influence others. While there are certainly influencers who are intelligent and who are subject matter experts, the proliferation of this trade has caused many in the younger generation who view influencing as a viable future profession, absent any education.

Education is not necessarily a college degree. It is not learning mathematics or mastering complex, specific subjects such as biochemistry or neurology. Instead, education is the critical thinking that is the taproot of success in any line of work irrespective of complexity. A person who has difficulty reading will be unable to pursue a career in law and a career in vehicle maintenance equally. If he cannot read, then he certainly cannot comprehend legal textbooks much less repair guides and manuals. Without that ability to read he cannot even undertake general life activities, such as purchasing a home, as he would be unable to read or understand the contract or undertake any employment that requires him to read and comprehend words critical to his job.

That is why education involves a broad spectrum of things that enable people to do other things. We have failed to realize that a good education is not just a college degree but also learning a trade. If a person who completes high school knows how to read, he does not necessarily have to spend tens of thousands of dollars to obtain a degree at a university, he could be just as well off if he were to undertake the process of learning a trade such as plumbing. As I was told during a Crisis in the Classroom town hall by a criminal lawyer about his brother repairing his pipes, he looked at the bill after the family and friends discount and, as a lawyer, second-guessed whether the countless hours he spent obtaining a legal degree and concurrently the pile of advanced degrees that come with the promise of high pay, really were all that worth pursuing if one only pursued them for monetary gain.

In other words, money can be made without a college degree by acquiring skills for which there is a high demand but a slender supply. The law of supply and demand at work. We are all born with different aptitudes.

It is the role of schools and our teachers to inculcate critical thinking and eschew indoctrination. Unfortunately, our teachers are underpaid and overworked and overstressed and underappreciated. Administrators often look to teachers as scapegoats for criminal activity to enrich themselves through deceit and cover-up.

Money, whether we like it or not, is the great equalizer. It incentivizes individuals to work harder and be more efficient in the furtherance of a future filled with the comfort and pleasures that money provides. Certainly, teachers should become teachers because they want to teach the next generation of leaders; however, internal morality and motivation can only take a person so far when they are destitute.

Teachers should be paid like CEOs; we should take

advantage of their desire to do good for their students and motivate them further by providing them with pay incentives based on their students' performances. We can be sure that there will be those who will cut corners and fudge numbers for extra pay, but we can be equally sure that those people will represent an infinitesimally small minority and that, with the proper safeguards put in place, the government can create a structure that holds those bad actors accountable.

One would think that with billions of dollars and yearly funding each school system would be able to pay their teachers not just a livable wage but a wage that allows them to live comfortably and will enable them to teach their students without stress. However, when speaking to a guest during one of my town halls, she concluded that although much money is given to school systems, far too much is squandered within their bureaucracies. In her eyes, there are generally far too many levels of bureaucracy in educational systems that force them to spend more and more money as more of it continues to be wasted every year.

Teachers' unions are to the education of students what a ball and chain are to a swimmer. Their counter-educational mission is the collective maximization of pay and benefits coupled with a collective minimization of work. Whether students learn is an afterthought, like an extra in a Cecille B. DeMille cinematic extravaganza.

Unionized teachers deplore excellence and extra effort because tacit aspersion is cast upon mediocrity or worse, which characteristically earmark all large organizations. The lowest common denominator prevails. The growth of teachers' unions corresponds to a decline in student learning. Although there are multiple causes of the vertical fall, teachers' unions are a prime culprit by removing monetary incentives for teaching excellence demonstrated by student achievement.

These unions have turned the profession of teaching from one of superior morality to one of profit-seeking. Union leaders have sued to prevent the opening of charter schools so that their union power is not threatened. The New York State United Teachers and the United Federation of Teachers sued to block a charter school from opening. While the teachers' unions spent thousands of dollars—if not hundreds of thousands—to prevent what is considered in this case to be an extremely prestigious school, New York City public schools continue to be plagued with high crime filled with below-the-poverty line students. In sum, money from the teacher's union is being used to block children's opportunities for a superior education compared to what is obtainable in public schools.

The National Education Association (NEA) and the American Federation of Teachers (AFT) are the chain and ball of education. The NEA sports a teacher membership of three million, assets approximating $370 million, and annual income and expenditures approximating $390 million. The corresponding figures for the AFT are 1.7 million teacher members, $100 million in assets, and annual income and expenditures approximating $200 million. Approximately 90 percent of public-school teachers belong to unions.

The pay, benefits, and other terms and conditions of employment of public-school teachers are set by elected public officials—typically in collective bargaining agreements with teachers' unions. It is thus unsurprising that the latter seek to curry favor with the former with handsome campaign contributions or lobbying. According to Open Secrets, the NEA's annual political contributions approximate $10 million, whereas the corresponding AFT figure approximates $4 million. The NEA's annual lobbying expenses exceed $2.5 million.

The self-dealing here is egregious. Public officials are inclined to generosity with taxpayer dollars to compensate unionized teachers in exchange for political support in the form of donations and votes. Student achievement be damned. Compulsory school attendance laws shield public officials and unions from accountability by guaranteeing a captive audience.

The power of teachers' unions finds expression in recurring illegal teacher strikes with impunity in New York, Chicago, Seattle, and elsewhere. Public officials are too intimidated to enforce the law. What a deplorable example for students who are the biggest losers and witness their teachers profiting from illegal activity.

Teachers' unions are implacably opposed to any measure

that would hold members accountable for their success in teaching, for example, pay for improving student performance whether on standardized tests or otherwise. It is altogether understandable that the NEA and AFT would do this. Their purpose is to hike teacher compensation and diminish teaching demands. But it is incomprehensible that elected officials would permit such a rip-off at the expense of hapless students. Can you imagine the owner of the New York Yankees paying the same salary to Babe Ruth and the bat boy? Elected officials tolerate teacher union maleducation to elicit campaign contributions. This must stop. Federal government contractors are prohibited from making contributions or expenditures, or promising to make any such contribution or expenditure, to any political party, committee, or candidate for federal office, or to any person for any political purpose or use. Corresponding prohibitions should be enacted by state and local governments for teachers' unions representing public school teachers.

The abysmal state of public-school education controlled by teachers' unions has given birth to private and charter schools as competitive alternatives for ambitious and industrious parents and students. That is all for the good. Monopoly is a narcotic and competition is a stimulant to learning. School voucher programs enabling parents to enroll their children in private schools and escape from public school captivity with no additional expense are wildly popular but are predictably fiercely opposed by teachers' unions.

In Washington, D.C. approximately 1,600 students receive vouchers of $8,000 for grades K-8 and $12,000 for high school. They graduate at higher rates than do their public-school counterparts, although per pupil expenditures for them per school year is substantially higher, soaring past $20,000. The mere existence of voucher programs is positive. Public schools are incentivized to improve performance to retain students.

The growth of voucher programs is stunted, however, because of political opposition ignited by teachers' unions and their campaign and voting clout. They are available to only a small percent of the 50 million public school students nationwide.

Publicly funded, privately operated charter schools also compete with the teachers' union-dominated public school system. Charter schools with various restrictions are authorized in forty-five states and the District of Columbia. They enroll 3.4 million students nationwide in more than 7,500 charter schools, compared with 100,000 public schools attended by 50 million students nationally. Teachers' unions implacably oppose charter schools to kill educational competition in the bud, which explains the substantial financial handicap under which the latter operates. Charter schools receive fewer dollars per pupil than district public schools.

Though there are year-to-year fluctuations, the average charter school receives 75 cents for every dollar the average district school receives.

Notwithstanding the limited availability of unsubsidized private schools, vouchers, and charter schools, the NEA and AFT through political clout guarantee public schools a more than 90 percent share of student enrollment—an educational monopoly by any measure that fosters indolence and stagnation.

There is a better way. State or local laws should authorize learners' unions to bargain with teachers' unions and elected officials over the school budget, curriculum, and terms and conditions of learning and teaching. In cases of impasse, an impartial arbitrator should be empowered to decide between competing alternatives proposed by the three parties. Learners' unions should receive public funds to retain necessary experts and legal advice. This concept of learner representation in education is no novelty. At least twenty-five states have students who sit on local school boards. But a student member is readily outnumbered. Learners' unions are necessary to rectify that imbalance.

Despite my disparagement of teachers' unions, it would be wrong to conclude that they are the serpent in an educational garden of Eden. Education is a complex undertaking and is influenced by multiple causes. If teachers' unions were outlawed, students would not turn instantly into Isaac Newtons or William Shakespeares and scale the intellectual heights. As H. L. Mencken observed, "Every complex problem has a solution which is simple, direct, plausible—and wrong."

What we are seeing in school districts across the country is a shift in priorities from student to administrator—not even to the educator. This shift in priorities is destroying neighborhoods and creating a generation of leaders that will be less educated and more corruptible. Our school systems and unions should not be working to profit in the short term, but they should view education as a long-term endeavor and give students access to as many educational opportunities as possible even if it comes at the expense of their bottom lines.

Without an educated and engaged public, the United States will not long endure. Education must be our number one priority. It creates the human capital more valuable than all the gadgets or creature comforts in the world. If we do not all hang together in the educational enterprise—teachers, administrators, parents, students, and public officials alike—then assuredly we will all hang separately. As Thomas Jefferson elaborated, "If a nation expects to be free and ignorant in a state of civilization, it expects what never was and never will be."

THE CRISIS OF INTELLIGENCE

Higher education is the lifeblood of progress. Students who attend universities have the opportunity to advance their level of thought and reasoning, as well as to pave new ground in fields of study that may be of use to our nations and our people. Unfortunately, going to college is no longer considered a luxury but rather an expectation. Because of this, many people in society now believe that getting a college degree is the only way to achieve financial success and have a profession that is satisfying. A conviction that, in the end, does damage to those who are most in need, notably minority groups.

Students are given the opportunity to engage in more and more useless majors, which leads to very low hiring expectations and low salary expectations, causing a massive cycle of debt that pushes down communities that can't afford them. As tuitions continue to rise to fill the pockets of their administrators and create unnecessary infrastructure to expand the school's power, students are given the opportunity to engage in more and more useless majors.

The corruption and thirst for power have become so obvious that we have come to accept it as the norm as both public and private universities compete for the best students, the best infrastructure, the most donations, and the highest administrator salaries. They do so by creating the perception that college is something that should be required, and they expand their concentration offerings to give the most amount of people the most opportunity to attend their schools and consequently increase that school's power.

As it turns out, the follies of market competition that charter schools are accused of misapplying to make more money and gain more power happen at a grander scale in public and private universities.

Minority groups are forced into a hole that they are unable to climb out of as a result of the inability to finance college without massive loans and the perception that gaining a high-paying job requires a college degree. To make matters even worse, in a desperate attempt to dig them out of the hole without giving up their precious dollars, schools provide these minority groups with incentives that are available only to them. Affirmative action policies embody the very idea that the road to Hell is paved with good intentions. These policies seek to force minority communities to skip the gradual progression that a historically underserved community needs to be better equipped both financially and intellectually to have the support to focus on studies and the ability to effectively learn.

Rather than constructing obstacles that can only be traversed by those with the requisite degree of intellect, we should instead focus on breaking down the payment walls. Doing so will give students motivation to work hard because they will have the knowledge that higher education will not be a risk that they may end up paying for the remainder of their lives, but an opportunity to better themselves and their communities. Those who excel academically in high school and are accepted to prestigious colleges won't have to face the agonizing decision of whether or not they should forego attending a better school that offers better career prospects simply because they don't have enough money to pay for it.

It is imperative that we come to the realization that even though a college education is necessary for society to go even further and become more knowledgeable in both our ability to solve problems and our comprehension of the world that surrounds us, it is not for everyone, and there are many other occupations that do not require a college degree that may be just as fulfilling and can pay just as much with equivalent or fewer hours of work. We must make an effort to break this norm and not allow our society to turn into a classist state. If we use college as a means to separate ourselves into classes, this will invariably serve only to compound the consequences that minority groups have faced as a result of years of poor policy aimed toward minority communities and their exploitation by powerful public officials.

For instance, students who attend trade schools may acquire the skills and information required to pursue careers in fields that are essential to the functioning of society. They can become capable of providing goods and services that everyone, even the wealthiest and most educated people among us, will invariably need, and will require on a regular basis.

In terms of career opportunities, particularly for under-served minority communities, trade schools frequently have private partnerships with major companies. These partnerships create a pipeline from the students' commencement ceremonies to employment opportunities after they have completed their education. The cost of obtaining those opportunities is low, the career prospects are high, and the salary, particularly when compared to the salary of the average person with a college education, is often the same or higher. Not only are the career prospects high, but the price to obtain those opportunities is low.

Because universities are offering a greater variety of con-centrations, students who choose to pursue one of these concentrations will be required to devote their lives to highly specialized fields of work that offer few opportunities after graduation and frequently function cyclically in which students who graduate end up teaching the field to students who then teach that field to new students.

Those members of underrepresented groups who are already struggling to make ends meet have no need to buy into the false promise of affluence that a college degree conveys. They don't need to put themselves in debt to the tune of tens of thousands of dollars just so they can go out and have fun and write papers whose sole purpose appears to be to enrich their minds in a very particular way, rather than providing them with general means of knowledge and new ways of thinking that will make them and their peers more successful.

This is not to imply that going to college is a waste of time or that it should be done away with altogether. The proliferation of employers, and consequently students who demand a college education because they believe that they will be more qualified, has created a system that encourages unnecessary debt accumulation as a result of receiving an unnecessary and often useless education. However, every system has its own flaws, and, fortunately, this is a flaw that we are able to correct. And if we do, we will be able to encourage students—particularly minority students—to pursue careers in trade schools and other similar types of schools that will offer them greater fulfillment, more money, and provide them with a job that they went to school for, as opposed to a job that they didn't go to school for.

Black graduates have, on average, $25,000 more in student loans than their white peers do after graduation. To be absolutely clear, this is not a negligible number when viewed in relation to the total amount that they borrow. The average amount of money that Black students owe in student loans is around $52,000. These startling numbers take on an even greater significance when one considers the fact that the average income of Black people is much lower than that of white people. So, on top of all the problems that Black and other minority communities face due to a history of discrimination and wrongful treatment against them, their futures are also placed in a stranglehold by massive debts that will take significantly longer to pay off than their white counterparts who can leverage their shorter time to pay their debt off to advance their careers and provide them with the ability to take more risks to improve their lives and the lives of their communities financially without having to worry about the repercussions of doing so.

Student debts have a negative impact not only on the ability to take risks and grow in one's profession but also on the ability to create a family and be able to financially raise a child and give them a comfortable life. According to one recent study, for instance, almost one-third of those who went to college said that they intended to postpone getting married in order to have their student loans paid off first. The decision to be married is an important one in life, especially when it comes to the subject of childrearing. It may take ten years or more to pay off student loans, representing a full decade during which a person could have been having one or more children and adding their skills and other abilities to the economy and the workforce. If a person has to wait that long to pay off their student loans, then they are missing out on those opportunities. This can lead to a standstill in minority communities, as fewer children with fewer resources and fewer opportunities grow up to become successful people. Instead, this stifling creates minorities who are dependent on the government for assistance and are unskilled laborers who contribute nothing to their communities or to the advancement of their race.

The problems that are found in higher education do not need to be remedied by increasing the number of opportunities available to Black children who are not qualified for the schools to which they are offered admission. Nor do these problems need to be remedied by wiping away student debt, which will inevitably be replaced by higher tuition and, as a result, more debt. Instead, we need to encourage Blacks and other minorities to use the foundational knowledge that they gained from preschool through high school, as well as the wisdom they will eventually find as they mature—the wisdom that will inevitably come to all of us—to create successful careers that bring opportunities and that advance their communities and enrich them with more money and more power.

THE CRISIS OF HOME LIFE

———

Education is the great equalizer. An educated man can stand in any salon with any group and reason as an equal no matter what his background or means.

Educational excellence is within reach for every family, regardless of socioeconomic status; an ethos of learning spread throughout a household is the key. Siblings and parents should read nonfiction and fiction brimming with moral tales to one another, such as *Uncle Tom's Cabin* and *Huckleberry Finn*. They should play word games such as Scrabble, write each other essays or poems, compete to see who reads the most each month, and discuss topics in the news.

These strides towards educational excellence are available to any household. The costs are *de minimis*. All that is needed are changes in attitude, discipline, and priorities.

Just about all of us who are either starting or long into our professional careers understand that learning is not confined to the classroom. It never sleeps. Each day we meet new people, we encounter new topics, and our learning expands.

Otherwise, our minds stagnate. And to paraphrase Socrates, a life with a stagnant mind is not worth living. Households must create an environment that is a stimulus not a narcotic to learning.

To do this, parents must set an example. According to Ralph Waldo Emerson, "Your actions speak so loudly, I can not hear what you are saying." Children must be taught how to write, as it is the most intellectually demanding of disciplines. A child can start with a daily task of one sentence, then maintain a protocol of writing daily paragraphs or diary entries until it becomes as enjoyable as any game. Eventually, they will learn not just to write, but to speak with felicity using words like "cluck" or "scamper," even at a young age that evoke images that keep the reader engaged. They can be taught to write using words that harmonize like a symphony orchestra to learn that prolixity is the father of boredom while brevity is the mother of memorable emotional and intellectual punch.

Television, video games, and the litany of new entertainment that is readily accessible to children and that dumbs down their minds should be either discouraged or banned from the household. Adults should know that entertainment is to learning what dessert is to the main course—a treat but not a necessity. Most of us work long hours to support ourselves. Entertainment is secondary and comes only if something more is left over. Children must be taught this same concept. Studies come first and entertainment comes only if that priority has been satisfied.

What if a child received fifteen minutes of entertainment for every hour that they read or write? That child would receive an allotment of one hour of television for every 125 pages of a book they read. Eventually, as the child reads more and more, and watches television or plays video games less and less, enjoyment will be derived more from reading and a growing knowledge base than from mindless fixation on a screen. The excitement of understanding will eclipse what the evanescent juvenile thrills of television and video games can offer. Yet, this environment and discipline are rarely present in minority households.

Literacy and reading must be promoted throughout minority communities more than ever before. Sir Francis Bacon advised, "Reading maketh a full man; conference a ready man; and writing an exact man."

All reasoning is by analogy. Practice, practice, and more practice are what is necessary to draw analogies. Communications talents are not a product of spontaneous generation. Michelangelo said, "Genius is eternal patience." He continued, "The greatest danger for most of us is not that our aim is too high, and we miss it, but that it is too low and we reach it."

Providing a household conducive to knowledge is one way to inspire a new generation to value learning and to improve itself through education.

The following are some suggestions for ways in which we could alter the customary images that greet you when you enter the house of a middle-class family in our nation. To begin, parents should seriously consider turning off the television unless the program they are watching is meant to educate, provide news, or discuss current events. I recognize the fact that as the second largest Black owner of television stations in the nation asking people to turn off their sets is profoundly ironic.

Of course, this does not mean that watching television, in general, is a negative thing. If you are viewing television intending to broaden your mental horizons, expand your intellect, and gain a more in-depth grasp of the most pressing topics of the day, then it is undeniably beneficial for you to do so. And, of course, indulging oneself for a moment is almost always healthy. Variety is the spice of life.

Your mind will almost certainly become more open if you make a habit of watching town hall meetings on the themes that are being discussed in our culture and society. Humans are social beings; as such, we learn from one another and broaden our horizons by listening to the experiences and viewpoints of others. Town halls, debates, and other structured forms of televised conversation can allow both adults and children to expand their perspectives by listening to the voices of people whom they will never meet and whose perspectives they will likely never hear—at least not until they are older. Used properly, television can expand horizons instantly without the costs and time necessary for travel.

But what do the majority watch on their televisions? Predominantly garbage or drivel. Reality television glorifies immorality and vainglorious consumption. Popular apps monitor every move made by well-known influencers who are famous for scandal or dissipation.

Especially regarding minority communities, these depraved diversions and models should be disavowed, not emulated. Is reality television really anything more than herding large groups inclined to squander time watching the antics of the ignorant whose sole role is to embarrass in front of a national audience?

A well-functioning, stable two-parent home is an incredible blessing for the kids. But in a culture that promotes "baby momma" and "baby daddy," this recognition is all too commonly overlooked. Statistics showing the deleterious effects on the Black community—especially young Black men who are incarcerated at shockingly high rates— are shocking. What makes for soaring television ratings may be toxic to real life.

By feeding viewers with conflict, fighting, and drama, high ratings are likely to follow. This is especially true for programming that airs on the small screen. Outrageousness easily trumps order.

You will quickly understand what I mean if you navigate

even fleetingly the content of almost any media platform. In our consumer-driven culture where everything is subservient to money, materialism rules the roost. In a culture that celebrates learning, in contrast, discretionary income is devoted to purchasing books and continuing education, investments that will pay off tenfold in the long run.

Visit the local mall. Count the number of youths who are wasting their time waiting in line to enter the Gucci store even without money for the extravagance on display. Observe sneaker stores that charge hundreds of dollars more for basically the same product—footwear with a rubber sole—that reap staggering profits because a Michael Jordan shoe is coveted as a status symbol. Such are the malign effects of the media.

Peek at the number of adolescents riding your local bus who are carrying Louis Vuitton handbags and backpacks. Look at their shoes. Which shoe design is now the most popular across the world? Products with exorbitant markups are sold by Kanye West and others like him, and Gucci slides, a pair of flip-flops with the brand Balenciaga or Fendi printed on them, are valued more than appreciating assets.

Such senselessness is fueled by the myopia of youths who discount long-run success. Even worse, the rampant materialism that has come to earmark a large portion of minority groups has encouraged consumption rather than investment. Flip-flops, backpacks, and a selection of designer clothes have no lasting value in contrast to a home, education degree, or blue-chip stocks or bonds. Young children from underrepresented groups are being led astray by the media into thinking that high fashion is as exclusive as diamonds. How you speak and your profession are far superior to clothes as symbols of success and achievement.

Survey the typical American house and count the number of books that line the bookshelves. How many bookcases do you think typical Black families have in their homes?

The answer is edifying. The typical white family home has 120 books, but the typical Hispanic family home and the typical Black family home only have seventy-nine and seventy-two books, respectively.

Fewer books and fewer ways for children to acquire knowledge means more indulging in mindless entertainment for the lack of anything better to do. But that is not all. Many very young children have smartphones, which, like television, video games, and other amusements, are a source of infinite distraction and preoccupation with drivel.

If, as Leo Tolstoy wrote in *Anna Karenina*, "All happy families are alike," similarly, all healthy households for children are the same. Race or ethnicity is irrelevant. At present, what differentiates minority culture are values inculcated in the home and educational encouragement. Reading a book has the same influence on the brain for all races. The brain is color-blind. But minority culture diminishes the likelihood that a book is read at all. Our brains do not have racial preferences.

The home should be a sanctuary of love and knowledge. It is optimal for imparting knowledge and values to a child. It is comfortable and familiar and enables intellectual exploration and discovery without the risk of embarrassment.

Moreover, in the home, a parent need not fear unscrupulous educators preaching a moral framework contradictory to their ideals of right and wrong. Parents are the commander-in-chief of the household. They can instruct and animate children far beyond the capabilities of traditional schools. A home environment conducive to learning works together with schools to endow children with the knowledge and inspiration required to surmount the gates of poverty and enter the domain of prosperity.

Archimedes said, "Give me a lever and I can move the world." Give children education and motivation for lifetime learning and the world will be their oyster.

However, in cities across the United States our children are failing; the result of poor leadership from those we entrust with one of the sacred duties of a civilization, and that is to prepare the next generation to lead and innovate to take the culture to the next stage of advancement, progress, and prosperity.

A recent Johns Hopkins University study showed that Baltimore city schools are failing in nearly every single category. Not only are children struggling to learn and get a quality education, but they are also forced to do so in unsafe and sometimes inhospitable environments that fail to meet the standards of schools in wealthier neighborhoods. Today, students enjoy luxuries that benefit their learning experience. Things like air conditioning, for example, were unavailable to students until the late twentieth century. Despite this, many inner-city schools lag behind; they are unable to even afford updated textbooks, let alone offer their students the same luxurious educational experience as schools in affluent, non-minority areas. Some schools are even filled with mold and have dilapidated structures and unusable facilities.

While we all know the challenges of school districts like Baltimore Public Schools, other cities across the country are also struggling to educate our students.

In Mississippi, the George Country District came under fierce scrutiny, and eventually probation, for multiple violations of the state's education rules after allegations surfaced that staff sanctioned cheating to pass students and get more dollars. An investigation into the allegations by the Mississippi Department of Education found twenty-four out of thirty-two serious violations.

In one instance, a student was pressured to take a test for another student to help him graduate. The school board was also a problem, assigning critical administrative duties to people other than the superintendent. The entire district is in complete disarray, but this seems to be par for the course for many inner cities and poor and struggling communities. It's less about the students and more about power and corruption from overzealous adults who are more concerned about their own influence and how they are perceived by the public over the true education of the kids they're responsible for educating.

It is not just Baltimore, it is cities all across the country that are struggling, putting kids in positions to not succeed. At the end of the day, it is the kids who lose and the government who wins by having more people to care for and rely on it. It is the kids who are ill-equipped to compete in a competitive world. It is the kids who will end up becoming non-productive members of society, filled with contempt for the very communities they live in. Why? The answer is quite simple: the adults tasked with educating them and empowering them to be the best versions of themselves failed them before they ever even had a chance to succeed, and that is a crisis of epic proportions—a systemic crisis that can only be solved by rooting out corruption, not by injecting more money into the system.

But let's rewind. Let us focus on the triumphs rather than the shortcomings. Amish communities provide one such instance of achievement. Their simple, disciplined way of living has fostered a culture of devotion and resilience. It imparts considerably more than worthless information that they will likely never use. Rather than learning the politically charged topics that current grade schools and colleges impose on their students, they teach them only the most important topics, such as reading, writing, and arithmetic. These children are taught discipline at an early age—to find pleasure in their work and to engage in that activity rather than wasting time indulging in entertainment. They are given the chance to use the foundational knowledge that their education provides them to expand their knowledge base through their life experience. They are given the opportunity to enjoy a life free from the stresses of the fast-paced, competitive American lifestyle that we impose on ourselves, yet still compete in the marketplace by manufacturing and selling their products, building and selling homes, opening restaurants, cultivating crops, and raising livestock.

The Amish are a religious community that live simply and traditionally. Though they are often the subject of ridicule due to their unconventional lives—riding horses and buggies, avoiding electricity and electrical devices—they are frequently the ones with the last laugh.

In many Amish communities, there is just one classroom and eight grades. That's all. They do not incur significant debt in order to utilize education as a formality for entry into life, nor do they spend years studying material they will never use in order to get a job that never needed a four-year degree in the first place. Instead, children labor and learn the value of hard work from an early age. They see life as a classroom and strive daily to improve themselves through their work, and they have a strong two-parent family structure to provide them with more stability and certainty throughout their childhoods.

Although the majority of Amish go only as far as

eighth grade, they are statistical outliers in terms of achievement. For instance, according to a study by sociologist Donald Kraybill, 95 percent of new Amish businesses were still operating after five years. Other studies show that, during a similar five-year period, only around half of the general population's businesses remained open. Even more remarkable is that, even after five years, this number of 95 percent is still much higher than the general population's rate of 82 percent after only one year in business. With flourishing enterprises come more opportunities for their offspring. Typically, children learn their parents' profession at an early age and eventually assume the mantle.

Even without a formal or extensive education, strong family life can lead to tremendous achievement. They do not squander time on television or video games because they do not have access to them, and they do not spend all of their hard-earned money on fashionable apparel and other material items. This is a benefit to them because they are not subjected to the artificial pleasures of society. Instead, they treasure their experiences, cherish those around them, and they strive as a community and family to achieve success in a world that, due to the high rates of post-degree unemployment, seems to be devoid of opportunity to the general population.

There are plenty of opportunities to go around; generational wealth can be built by promoting hard work and not time-wasting or indulgence. When family, education, and discipline are respected, they build value and give an education experience unequaled by conventional schools. It is not artificial like formal education; rather, it is genuine education in its purest form.

2021: Crump in a moment of solitude.

2021: Crump and the Reverend Al Sharpton knelt in solidarity in front of the courthouse where the police officer accused of killing George Floyd was on trial.

ESSAYS BY
BENJAMIN CRUMP, ESQ.

THE CRISIS OF DEATH

Ben Franklin said that Democracy is akin to two wolves and a lamb voting on what to have for lunch. It doesn't take a genius to know the outcome of that vote. But he then profoundly declared that Liberty is a well-armed lamb contesting the vote. It is our solemn obligation to make certain that young Black lambs are adequately armed to protest the school-to-prison pipeline. Well-armed does not entail any means of violence; no bullets, firearms, and the like. We must equip them with intellect, strategic thinking, a moral compass, and a quality education. This is the only way for them to resist becoming part of the school-to-prison pipeline that claims and destroys too many of our youth.

Black children do not need to be martyrs for their communities. There is a disturbingly high rate of violent crime in a sizable portion of Black communities across the United States. Their despair appears to have no end in sight, and the generations of families who live in these communities are caught in a cycle of poverty and criminality. They are forced to deal with the consequences of being the wrong color in the wrong neighborhood. There is no obligation for Black children to give their lives for the sake of their communities. Yet, many Black children find themselves victims of unnecessary violence—isolated from the access and opportunities, at no fault of their own, that children in other communities so frequently enjoy. The very essence of childhood is stripped away, forcing children to think about things only adults should have to contend with; survival mode quickly kicks in, and whatever innocence they may have had quickly dies with the harsh reality of the life and environment they're forced to live.

In the absence of quality education, a significant number of Black children who are subjected to these educational systems resort to criminal activity as the only way to improve their circumstances and make a better life for themselves. It is simple for those who are well-off and well-educated to look at gang violence and other forms of crime through their own lens, and they may find it amusing to consider the possibility that anyone could think it reasonable to put their lives in danger every day in order to make a living. When we put ourselves in the position of a child growing up in a poor neighborhood, surrounded by death and crime, and forced to go through an educational system that does not care about their success, it's easy to see how crime becomes not just a choice, but a way of life. Simply put, for so many young Black children, the odds of success seem automatically against them.

The psychological toll this has on our young Black kids is devastating. The feeling of invisibility and the madness that comes from attending a poor public school that will only lead to a life of poverty in adulthood is a conundrum. The onslaught of murder, crime, and continuous poverty, coupled with failing public school systems have lead to a litany of emotional trauma that very few other kids experience. The toll of this trauma and how it leads to anxiety and aggression, as psychology professor Dawn Henderson notes, leads to an unhappy place for many poor Black children.[1]

The conundrum that frequently arises is as these children become young men and women, they are severely limited in their ability to do anything beyond working a menial minimum wage job.

Imagine seeing the success of others and wondering about the opportunities afforded elsewhere, yet severely lacking in every regard around you. If an individual works for minimum wage, they can maintain a lifestyle that is both impoverished and relatively sustainable. However, when one lives in a nation that provides us with a great deal of potential, it is dangerous to become complacent. This is because, as

---

1   Dawn X. Henderson, "The Mad and Unhappy Place of Public Education for Black and Brown Children in the United States." Psychology Benefits Society, October 1, 2015, https://psychologybenefits.org/2015/10/01the-mad-and-unhappy-place-of-public-education-for-black-and-brown-children-in-the-united-sates/. Accessed September 13, 2022.

one stays complacent, the world improves around you, and inevitably you will end up stuck in a worse position than you started.

There is possibility that when these underprivileged young Black adults turn on their televisions or scroll through social media and see the luxuries that others enjoy, there is a sense of inferiority. Albeit, there is nothing inferior about them, but the lack of opportunities, which is no fault of their own. As a result, acquiring luxury items in order to imitate the lavish lifestyles and fashions of the rich and famous becomes a requirement rather than a desire.

Who, if anyone, is to blame for the anguish and frustration they have to endure, the prolonged trials that drive them to seek refuge in criminal activity? Surely, we cannot blame children for the poverty that exists in their environment and the lack of resources and opportunity that kills their dreams and desires before they can ever see any possibility of them coming to fruition.

Our suffering is the direct result of a system that does not support Black children and places a higher value on financial gain than it does on morality. Existing within our organizations' bureaucracies and administrators, these individuals place an emphasis on themselves and the growth of their power at the expense of the children they have accepted the responsibility to serve. They have created a system that rewards failure above all else and recognizes superficial calls for change more so than actual action. They have designed this system to incentivize failure. We have put our faith in people who cannot be relied upon, and we have been indifferent as they have brought our communities to their knees while we have stood by and done nothing. Far too many of our children have failed and have seen their dreams unrealized. We must foster an environment where education flourishes and provides our children with the best resources available for them to ascertain the future each of them deserves.

These individuals who cause harm to our children create conditions that result in a deleterious impact on their future and ours as a community. Those who seek to politicize and marginalize our children should be placed squarely in our sights and held accountable for their actions and inactions, and we should make sure they are aware that we are watching their every move, ensuring they will be held accountable for their actions if they stray away from their duties.

The children that they put through the system and profit from either will become leaders or subjects, and this will be determined by the level of success or failure that the system achieves. When Black communities are unfairly targeted for profiteering, it is inevitable that those of other races will lead in the future. Whether it be African Americans, Hispanics, or any other minority group that has been unfairly exploited by powerful government figures, the future will be led by those of other races. Although many public figures and members of the media have stated publicly that they support the advancement of underrepresented groups into positions of power, very little has been done to make this goal a reality.

Because I understand that the fight for education is not just a fight for the betterment of a few lives, but a fight for the future of America—a fight that will determine whether or not our future leaders will represent us all, I have joined a lawsuit against the City of Baltimore for their failure of the children in Baltimore. I joined this fight for equity, I joined this fight to be a voice for children and families who don't have the wealth and power to speak for themselves. I joined this fight because our children deserve the same opportunities as every other child in America, and it is time to demand that cities across this country step up and deliver on their promise of a good and quality education for all children.

As citizens of the United States of America, it is our sacred obligation to fight sin wherever it manifests itself and to seek absolution for the transgressions of those who came before us. It is possible that we could become a better nation if we admitted our shortcomings and sought reparation for the suffering caused by people in this generation as well as those who came before us. No one ever wants to acknowledge their shortcomings, including entire nations, I get it, but acknowledgement is a key component of addressing problems and for far too long we've ignored the problems that have plagued Black children.

It is of the utmost importance to focus on acts of Black-on-Black violence because they are responsible for the untimely deaths of a large number of young and impressionable Black people. Tragically, gang violence has become pervasive throughout Black communities. Even though the negative impact that gang violence has seems to defy reason, there is no question in anyone's mind as to why it continues to spread. Violence is never the answer, and we as Black, specifically those of us who are men, must think about how we can step up to mentor young boys early enough to guide them on the right path. We also have to reach out to our young men and teach them a better way—that is our responsibility and no one else's. With that said, the government does play a role, and the proliferation of illegal guns has wreaked havoc on the lives of too many in our community. Gangs use them as their go-to tool to instill fear and violence against other gangs from neighboring communities and sometimes against innocent people in their own communities.

Our children are left feeling unsafe in schools, sometimes in their own homes, and in the community. Where are Black children safe? This is a question I often reflect on, and the fact that I even have to ask is depressing enough, but it also reminds me of why we must improve the state of our communities for the sake of our children. They deserve every opportunity possible, and in their search of self-discovery, we must afford them an environment to explore all of their God-given talents.

The desire to become a member of a gang is almost always driven by purely mechanical considerations. If a person is incapable of fending for him or herself, does not have a stable family or support structure, and is at an impressionable age, then this means that their lives will be completely devoid of any critical structure, which would necessitate the need for them to join a gang to provide that structure. Structure is key for kids and instills discipline and expectations that children need. It also goes further, it creates an environment for children to feel safe, comfortable, and free to be themselves—and it is our responsibility as adults to curate and ultimately foster that environment.

It is unfortunate that anyone would join a violent gang; however, we can take some solace in the fact that this problem, which primarily affects neighborhoods inhabited by minorities, can be rectified by improving our educational system. I am confident that if given support, and access to opportunities, a great majority of our young people would choose to pursue their dreams.

We won't have to increase the size of our police departments or create additional anti–gang violence units. As a result, we won't have to throw away billions of dollars on the war on drugs or imprison young Black children who are responsible for selling illegal substances. Instead, these resources could be put to better use by assisting people who are struggling financially and whose problems can be solved with additional financial support. Redirecting resources for more purposeful and meaningful impacts will have a lifelong and generational impact on the Black community and the nation as a whole. These investments aren't merely for the appeasement or atonement of Black people, but for the entire country.

Those who join gangs do so in the hopes of finding a family with whom they can share their most personal experiences and a safe haven from the outside world. Their connection is frequently as powerful as that of blood. It should not come as a surprise, given the high percentage of single motherhood that exists in Black communities, that a significant number of Black children require the assistance of an additional family member, or even an entire unit, in order to provide them with a support system. Ultimately, if a Black child grows up in a family with only one parent and that parent needs to work multiple jobs to support them, then the child will be forced to deal with the difficulties associated with constructing a moral framework without the guidance of a second parent who has experienced life.

If children do not receive an education, they will almost never have the opportunity to pursue a meaningful career that they find enjoyable or that provides them with the sufficient financial stability to lift themselves out of poverty. This makes it impossible for them to support themselves. Black children often have very limited access to steady sources of income; therefore, it is possible that Black children who join or aspire to join gangs do so in order to locate a group of people who may give them some stability in their lives. A form of shared suffering in which a group of people who are unable to maintain themselves can find support from others who are in a similar position to themselves. This is the opposite of what we want for our children. Collectively with our shared resources we can provide launching pads for Black children to aspire bigger than gangs, as every other kid in America. Knowing the support and systems are in place to help our kids when they struggle without rebuke, while encouraging them to keep soaring puts Black children on a pathway of success.

The acquisition of the knowledge and abilities required to differentiate between what is right and wrong, what is moral and what is immoral, as well as understanding the consequences of one's actions, is an essential component of education. Education has the ability to instill a sense of predictability in one's behavior. Those who have received a good education are aware of the consequences of possessing large quantities of illegal substances as well as the low probability of evading justice after committing a murder. However, a person who is raised on the streets and is unable to comprehend the immorality of murder will also be unable to comprehend the consequences of murder. This is because the two concepts are inextricably linked. In addition, because they were unable to differentiate between their knowledge of previous criminal arrests and the complexities of the investigations, they may have also been led to believe that they had a high likelihood of escaping punishment for their actions. This, in turn, leads to more people engaging in harmful behavior as a direct result of their lack of education.

What would happen if we made sure that every child and adult in our communities had access to high-quality educational opportunities? To begin, there will be fathers present who, under normal circumstances, would have given up their child along with the mother. These fathers would gain an understanding, as a result of their newly acquired education of the immorality of abandoning a child and the sense of obligation they must undertake to become stronger allies of the child's mother and the child, as well as of their communities. Children need their parents and while so many Black women lift the burden alone, it's a norm that we must demand change.

The examples set by both mother and father makes a difference, and while perfection doesn't exist in anything, it is the best way to instill the values and support our children need. Frankly, it's the structure that is needed to raise children into young people equipped to tackle the problems of the world, and while every family dynamic is unique and different, we want to encourage what will not only have the greatest result for children, but also the parents. In addition, they will gain an understanding of the sense of obligation they must undertake to become stronger allies of their communities. They will view faith and wisdom as two sides of the same coin, and they will rely on their own knowledge as well as their devotion to their God in order to act responsibly toward their families.

The child will be brought up by two parents and will receive profound wisdom from them; he will be able to use his parents as moral guideposts or as a starting point for determining the path he will take in life. If a child has parents who are there for them when they need care and support, then that child will learn to appreciate the repercussions of even the most inconsequential of his actions. The child will have the opportunity to pursue a profession that is both personally satisfying and financially rewarding, and he will be able to provide for himself, his future family, his community, and eventually even for his own parents.

When education is brought into Black communities that are in danger, it will put an end to Black-on-Black violence. This is because Black men and women will no longer have any reason to engage in violent behavior when they no longer have any incentive to do so. They will be able to obtain a varied and structured moral conscience, and they will have a plethora of opportunities open to them. They will eventually come to the realization that the possibility of all of their hard work being wasted or of having to bear the repercussions of crime will be too great for them to continue engaging in criminal activity. In an ideal world, if given support and resources, I'm confident many young Black youths would choose a different route because they would have something to look forward to. The happiness of knowing they are pursuing their dreams, the happiness of knowing they too have the potential to be something great. I once heard this quote, "only those who dream the impossible can make the impossible commonplace." Well, we want Black children to dream as big as they can and to have everything they need to pursue those dreams and make them commonplace. The pursuit alone can be inspirational, challenging but necessary. I know that given that alternative between a life of crime or a life of hard work, with the proper support mechanisms in place, our children will choose the latter.

When evaluated from a risk-reward perspective that is more objective, the benefits that education bestows upon individuals residing in minority communities and the potential for change become more apparent. If the potential net gain from engaging in the illegal activity is greater than the potential net gain from refraining from the illegal action, then the likelihood of the individual engaging in the illegal activity will increase. We can only depend on faith and morality to a certain extent; when hopelessness becomes too overwhelming, even the noblest individuals among us may succumb to its torments.

The dissemination of knowledge has the potential to easily tip the scales and make the maintenance of lawfulness significantly more profitable than the maintenance of lawlessness.

When a person has the skills and education necessary to advance their careers or entrepreneurial endeavors, the cost of engaging in illegal behavior will be the amount of effort that they put in to get to that point, as well as the opportunity cost that they incur by forgoing further rewards that lawful behavior brings them. In other words, the cost of engaging in illegal behavior will be greater than the cost of engaging in lawful behavior. In the blink of an eye potential is thrown out of the window because the wrong decision was made, and for Black children the punishment is usually harsher and not as easily forgiven. We must fight that, but while we fight it, we must also teach the importance of doing right because you can never go wrong when doing right, but wrong deeds will always eventually catch up to us. It takes one mistake to ruin a life, a family, and community forever.

On the other hand, when one lacks the resources necessary to achieve success in the outside world, the advantages of engaging in illegal behavior frequently outweigh the advantages of acting in accordance with the law. To put it another way, if a person does not have access to education, the option of leading a lawful life is fraught with peril. Since lawfulness without education provides few personal benefits, and criminality without education often does, it is an ironic twist that society has no choice but to acknowledge it. However, we don't have to accept it because the future of our children is too vital.

Those who decided to take a leap of faith and dedicate themselves to living a lawful life have generally reaped the rewards and served as an example to encourage minority youth across the country and in their communities to leave the streets, quit the gangs, and choose a life of righteousness over a life of depravity. Those who decided to take a leap of faith and dedicate themselves to living a lawful life have generally reaped the rewards. Life is challenging enough and it's even harder with a criminal record, and more often than not this is overlooked by young and impressionable young people who yearn for a sense of belonging anywhere they can get it.

We will no longer be a protected people but rather a policed people if the Black community is unable to take that leap of faith and get an education, and we must stop limiting what success looks like. Not everyone will be a rapper, football player, or basketball player. For example, I shared a video on my social media of Dr. Jawanza Kunjufu in the late eighties speaking about the importance of education, and he cited this example: "There were a million Black boys last year who wanted to play in the NBA, of that million only four hundred thousand will make it to play high school ball, of that four hundred thousand only four thousand will make it to play college ball, of that four thousand,, only thirty-five will make it to the NBA, of that thirty-five, only seven start, and the average life in the NBA is four years, so the problem is we have a million brothers looking for seven full-time jobs that last four years. Yet, last year we had a hundred thousand jobs available to be a computer programmer, engineer, or doctor and only a thousand brothers qualified. So, our appeal to Black males is to realize the odds, that you do most, you do best." His words here are profound because we need to start thinking strategically about what's necessary to give our Black children the greatest odds of being successful. It is not enough to merely expect better resources and support, but we must also have better expectations about pathways to success.

It is common knowledge that crime is rampant in low-income Black neighborhoods, that the murder rate is through the roof, and that the number of people who have been victimized by criminal activity in these areas is incalculable. There is a requirement for more police presence in these Black communities because there is such a high rate of criminal activity there. Throughout the course of my career as a civil rights attorney, I have observed that the greater the number of police officers in a given area, the higher the probability that a Black person will be subjected to injustice at the hands of the police.

As a result, not only the criminals who attacked their communities but also the innocent become victims of the police as a consequence of increasing police presence. Ultimately, it turns out that the injustices committed by police can be indirectly linked to poor areas in general, regardless of race. This is the case because poor education is the root cause of poverty.

In the United States, we recognize that injustice against one person is an injustice against everyone, yet we take no action to stop the commission of such wrongs. Instead, we encourage criminal behavior, increase the number of police officers on the street, witness injustice, and then protest that injustice, causing the cycle to continue.

We need to find a solution to the disproportionately high crime rates that are found in Black areas. Education has the potential to break this cycle; it can reduce both criminal activity and the need for police presence at the same time. Black communities will no longer have the feeling that they need to fear law enforcement, and they can have the potential to significantly shift the relationship between the two groups.

Putting an end to violence committed by Blacks against other Blacks is a straightforward undertaking. The problem could be solved by determining the underlying factors that contribute to violent behavior. Individuals are harmed as a result of the racial prejudice that exists in our government institutions, and racism is still prevalent in our country. However, these issues might be resolved if more Black men and women were to hold positions of authority in the country. We still haven't made progress in boardrooms in New York City or the tech giants in Silicon Valley and it's time for that to change. With real power comes the ability to direct change. Providing Black men and women with educational opportunities is the first step toward elevating them to positions of power. Their climb to a better future and our shared goal of establishing a nation that is governed by people of all races will both be impossible to accomplish if they do not receive an education of sufficient caliber.

THE CRISIS OF MISINFORMATION

Our global community is now more interdependent than it has ever been. An idea has the potential to spread to every corner of the globe in an instant. Because of this newfound ability, for the first time in human history, each of us has the potential to disseminate and share our knowledge with people all over the world. We are no longer constrained by the volume of our voices or the speed of our wheels; rather, we are only restricted by the speed and availability of our internet connection, which is a service that is easily accessible to nearly everyone at a minimal price.

Nevertheless, with this power comes the responsibility to promote responsible ideas and to encourage compassion rather than hatred. The internet's pseudo-anonymity has, unfortunately, given a boost not only to sensible and benign ideas but also to ideas that promote hatred and intolerance.

Since the advent of the internet, we have come to realize that the convenience of communication combined with the physical separation of those who are interacting with one another causes the conversation to frequently deteriorate into the most morally reprehensible forms. People we have never met look down on each other, and powerful figures spew hateful opinions in the name of protecting their right to say them.

With the ability to communicate ideas, we can, of course, also listen to ideas. Unfortunately, a significant portion of the information that people read and comprehend is, to some extent, false.

It is not difficult at all to be led astray; in fact, even the most intelligent people among us are susceptible to being fooled, not just occasionally but frequently. There is no doubt that the vast majority of people have been in situations in which they have come across false or misleading information and believed it without conducting any additional research.

This phenomenon is destructive to society as a whole, but it is even more destructive to individuals who are unable to differentiate between fact and fiction and who are easily deceived by misleading information. It is simple for a person to believe in untruths when they lack the tools necessary to evaluate the world around them, and bad actors who propagate false information have more and more easy targets to take advantage of as a result.

Education not only provides us with an understanding of the content of the subject being taught, but it also shifts the way that we think about the world. For instance, the majority of lawyers are familiar with the phrase "think like a lawyer," which describes how lawyers should approach problems. Law students read cases and are exposed to competing opinions throughout the entirety of their time spent in law school. It often becomes impossible to choose a victor for any of these debates. Law students develop a new way of thinking as a result, and gain the ability to analyze and consider issues from a variety of points of view. The sum of their work allows them to use their newfound abilities to value perspectives that differ from their own, which can enable them to understand something with which they do not personally agree.

Education in fields such as nursing and engineering can shift one's perspective in a manner analogous to how attending law school can reorient one's way of thinking. But these are specialties. A fundamental education, on the other hand, is something that is given to us starting when we are young, and in the same way that these specializations can change the way you think, so can basic education. In fact, without a basic education, it becomes impossible to undertake any specialty. Because of the way it instructs us to think, school prepares us to be intellectual; it teaches us to question the things that aren't meant to be questioned and to discern and solve issues quickly as they arise.

There is a prolonged crisis in education as a nation and there is a growing possibility that people who spend time online will be exposed to false or misleading information. Thus, as there are more people online and more uneducated people, the likelihood that they and others will be taken advantage of as those numbers increase.

Sadly, this is not merely a hypothesis. Because there is a demand for it, fake news and hatred are spreading rapidly across the internet. Because there are enough people willing to believe falsehoods, this tactic used by political operatives, foreign nations, and domestic disruptors has been and will continue to be an effective strategy for shaping the perspectives of a significant portion of the population.

Even though any community can be and often is a victim of false and misleading news, communities with lower levels of education may be significantly more affected than those with higher levels of education. Misinformation has caused considerable harm to members of underrepresented groups. It has motivated Black people, who are already more likely to engage in criminal behavior as a result of their impoverished state, to commit crimes, both in general and against people of other races.

According to the findings of a 2020 study that was carried out by the University of Kansas, the level of education that an individual possesses is a reliable indicator of whether or not he or she will believe a specific piece of false information. In addition, the findings of the study suggested that groups of people are more likely to believe false information when it concerns a topic in which they have a personal stake.

It breaks my heart when I watch videos of Black men and women engaging in racial profiling, assaulting other people, and committing other crimes in general—especially when those videos go viral on the internet. This lack of education, which led to the occurrence of these crimes in the first place, clearly leads to an increase in racism and hatred against Blacks as the internet becomes increasingly flooded with depictions of blacks committing heinous crimes. They become caricatures and fodder for racists to use to justify their hatred for Blacks.

As a consequence, it is irrefutable that the educational systems that failed Blacks and caused them to become impoverished also contribute to their being considered as inferiors and criminals by people online. Unfortunately, this perception bleeds over into racist behavior in the real world, leading to an uptick in hate crimes and racist actions by people all around the country.

By providing Black people with access to high-quality educational opportunities, we can break this cycle. Education will indeed make it possible for people who live in impoverished areas to access the internet in a secure manner and prevent them from falling victim to unscrupulous people who spread misleading information. With the right kind of education, Black people will be able to recognize the distinction between fact and fiction when researching something online and will be less likely to victimize people of other racial groups. And third, Black people will not be caught on camera assaulting other people because they will understand the gravity of their behavior and refrain from doing it in the first place.

Crippling this cycle will lead to empowerment and advances for Black people across the United States. It will lead to economic advances desperately lacking in a majority of Black communities while awakening a sense of purpose and aspiration about the future. The goal and expectations are clear; now we need to foster it, and education is there to open that door.

This cycle will come to an end, which will be beneficial to the reputation of the Black community. Racists and other bigots will no longer have the ammunition they need to justify their antipathy toward Black people and encourage others to share their views.

Not all instances of hatred are caused by erroneous information; rather, some instances of hatred are caused by internal biases as well as other factors that motivate people. However, the ability to disseminate hateful material online has the chilling effect of increasing animosity towards Blacks. Additionally, it causes nearly everyone who encounters actual misinformation to accept it without inquiry because it reinforces their preconceived notions and beliefs.

Sadly, members of other races are not the only ones who contribute to this perception; members of the Black community are frequently the ones who do so as well. Celebrities, particularly rappers who make their lack of education public and use their status as powerful individuals to persuade Black people to hold views that are objectionable, are significant contributors to internet racism, despite the fact that misinformation is the primary factor in this form of racism. Black men and women look up to them as role models, and as a result, they tend to follow every word they say, which, unfortunately, frequently involves illegal substances and violent behavior.

People can learn values from role models in ways that they cannot from others. The natural likening and gravitating toward a person on a child's own accord compels them to take the messages of their role models more seriously than those of other people, even despite our feelings about family bonds and parental empowerment over our child's thought processes. These lyrics and online conduct become more than words; they become messages, and they turn a person into what they falsely believe that they should aspire to be.

The music that people listen to has a profound effect on who they are; it alters their vocabulary, the way that they dress, and their general attitude towards the world. This is something that we see reflected frequently in the perspectives of a great number of children and adults. Worse yet, these attitudes often go further than just how some individuals

carry themselves; rather, they lead to the children committing acts of violence in pursuit of being the person their role
model tells them to be.

Who else can a child turn to for help if they grow up
in a poor household and do not receive an education? In
fact, how could they go to anyone else if they are unable
to differentiate between a positive and negative example of
a role model? A child is more likely to seek advice from a
person who came from the same background, as opposed to
someone who came from a completely different background.
Because many of these rappers who promote violent messages started out in abject poverty and worked their way up
to fame as a result of their talents, it is only natural that
many young people would look up to them as a Sherpa to
help them climb out of their misery and achieve their goals.

It is abundantly clear that music plays a significant part
in the manner in which many people carry themselves; of
course, this is not restricted solely to rap music. But of course,
if the behavior in which a person engages in the name of
their musician role models is harmless, there is no problem,
and the behavior should be encouraged. The problem arises
when the actions of individuals can bring significant harm
to either themselves or others.

No government should ever require artists to use their
platform for good. That would be a violation of our right
to uninhibited speech. Instead, encouraging the spread
of a positive message should always take precedence over

mandating it. However, artists, and particularly rappers, who use their platforms to spread harmful messages should always be encouraged to be more cognizant of the impact that they have on the people who listen to them. These rap artists need to realize that while individuals are ultimately responsible for the choices they make, they also have a responsibility not to spread messages that encourage people who are easily influenced and already inclined to engage in risky behavior to do so in the first place. After all, it is not as if messages of copious drug use, the assault of women, murder, or using any illegal means to make money were the mainstream throughout history; that message has never been the one that was necessary to create hit songs, and it does not need to be today.

In every part of ourselves exists the part of another—a lesson learned, and a message received is another building block for ourselves. Artists should do better and ensure that the part of them that influence the lives of impressionable children is a positive one that will guide them to do great things in the future, not kill or harm one another.

And this is true for everyone who sends a message online: whatever they say will invariably be viewed by others, and it is likely that what they say will have an effect on them. It is not necessary for the influences to be immediate; rather, it can be a part of a larger stream of information that gradually alters a person's perception of the world. It is far too easy for someone to be inundated with sufficient messages that promote hatred and criminality thanks to the volume of content that is sent online every day. As a result, they may eventually come to accept those values and adopt them as their own after being exposed to enough of these messages.

Even worse, the algorithms used by social media platforms do not help improve the situation. No longer do social media platforms use feeds that are based on the passage of time. Feeds are based on interests in order to provide users with a more satisfying experience, to encourage users to remain on the social networking site, and to provide users with only the content that the algorithm believes they want to see. This can be useful in some ways, such as allowing us to view content that is tailored to our preferences, but it also has the potential to be harmful, and it is very likely that it will result in significantly more negative effects than positive ones.

Inclination is the decisive factor in interest in the long run. If a person has a history of positively reacting to a particular piece of content, then showing them that content will encourage them to stay and watch more of that type of content in the future. If an individual is predisposed to believe in hateful messages, this virtually constant cycle of content that we are predisposed to like being shown to us has the potential to inflict significant harm on that individual. When this occurs, the individual who is filled with hatred is shown messages that promote hatred rather than messages that promote unity. They are put in an environment with people who share their views, known as an echo chamber, and as a result, they are denied the opportunity to voice their disagreement.

While I was working as an attorney for the family of George Floyd, yet another unarmed Black man to be killed by police, I saw online propagation of divisive falsehoods by bad actors. People attempted to demonstrate that George Floyd and other unarmed Black males who had been killed by police, such as Eric Garner and Trayvon Martin, were in some way responsible for what had happened to them by drawing comparisons between the two sets of victims. They painted Mr. Floyd as a thug who either deserved it morally, got what he deserved as a result of his actions, or was at the very least apparently responsible for having an adult male kneel on his neck with his full body weight as he cried out for help. They did this by portraying him as a criminal. It became clear that the offensive comments could only have spread as far as they did because social media platforms like Facebook and Twitter made it possible for them to do so.

The proliferation of social media and the havoc it has caused in undereducated Black communities is both a blessing and a curse. It has misguided many people and caused many others to believe in narratives that are not factual. If we want to do the most good for Black communities, we should educate them and empower them to be vigilant online and against the never-ending cycle of criminality that causes them to be viewed as lesser people. This will ensure that they do not become a statistic, that they are not ridiculed online, and that they are not viewed as criminals because of the color of their skin.

THE CRISIS OF ENTREPRENEURSHIP

The United States of America is often regarded as the world's foremost entrepreneurial nation. Because of the government's business-friendly environment, the United States is home to many of the world's most successful and smartest businesspeople, many of whom were born and raised here and many who moved here from another country in search of prosperity. Anybody, regardless of race or ethnicity, is capable of starting a business and becoming their own boss if they have access to sufficient resources. On the contrary, the Black population has traditionally been denied access to opportunities like these. The potential that becoming an entrepreneur has for those who are interested in business has been diminished in Black communities. Because so many people lack the fundamental knowledge and business acumen essential to launch a profitable company, any ideas they come up with are bound to fail before they ever get off the ground.

A persistent education crisis has had and will continue to have an unequal effect on minority communities in a country that is supposed to provide hope for a better future—a country in which people are able to rise out of poverty in just one generation even if they start from nothing. As a result of this crisis, minority communities will not be able to see the hope that this country provides, nor will they be given the opportunity to rise out of poverty, and they will be forced to continue to live on the terms of another with little to no means of escape.

My role as a civil rights attorney requires me to have an understanding of the predicament of the individuals I defend. My experience has led me to the conclusion that the neighborhoods that are devoid of entrepreneurial spirit are the ones that are most often subjected to violent civil rights abuses. They have not been given the gift of creating wealth and owning assets; instead, they are compelled to work jobs that lead nowhere, jobs that are intended only to be undertaken by young people who are just starting out in their careers; jobs that pay a wage that is not sufficient to live by, jobs that offer few benefits, and jobs that offer few opportunities for career advancement.

These communities suffer from a mental fog caused by the sickness of complacency and acceptance of one's present condition. They are sick and hungry, but willing to endure the suffering because suffering is all they know. They have become consumed by their environments and the idea of anything beyond the walls of poverty is unimaginable, they are mere shadows on a wall beyond reach and actualization. Only those who can see the impossible can make that impossible commonplace, but when you cannot see success or opportunity one can never reach it.

When compared to communities that have strong educational systems and support for even those who do not care or who are failing, these minority communities lack the entrepreneurial spirit that encourages career growth and mentally punishes complacency. It is precisely this entrepreneurial spirit that infects the mind of those who have or have not found success in their lives, which makes even the successful who have stagnated crumble if they do not make an effort to improve their lives. It is this infection that has failed to spread throughout communities of color and compel success in the minds of everyone.

The fact that many of those who start their own businesses seldom, if ever, see a profit from their efforts is one of the primary reasons why minority communities absolutely must encourage and support entrepreneurial endeavors. The act of entrepreneurship, in and of itself, benefits people who surround the entrepreneur and generates income and opportunities for those who are part of the community of the entrepreneurs. This benefit can come directly or indirectly, yet, in any case, it always comes when the entrepreneur invests in his or her community. It is the key to ownership and generational wealth, in which Black Americans lag significantly behind our white counterparts. Black people live in communities and neighborhoods that we do not own. We have long struggled to see the realization of transferable wealth that other communities, notably white ones, enjoy, but we can change that through ownership.

However, it does not end with ownership; we have to also prioritize support of said ownership in order to foster growth and expansion. We are quick to support other entrepreneurs' dreams by supporting their businesses as consumers but need to engrain in our children that we need to support each other in the same capacity.

No matter what kind of business is established, whether it is a humble storefront or a cutting-edge technology startup, we can be certain that limitless opportunities will emerge as a direct consequence of the new venture. However, despite the fact that these opportunities are few in minority groups due to the crisis in education, there is another problem that often crops up in conjunction with the education crisis. The issue of flight.

There is always a flight of more educated minorities from their impoverished, crime-ridden neighborhoods towards ones that are safer and more prosperous. This is often caused by the absence of educated people in these communities. This deprives the communities that are responsible for raising future entrepreneurs and educated residents of an opportunity that could have been theirs; it gives these opportunities to strangers who may not have faced the same challenges simply because they received an education that led to their success. Many Black neighborhoods are at a disadvantage as issues arise, and we don't have enough highly skilled people to address those issues.

As a result of this, minority communities are left behind and forced to contend with the fact that, due to their poor educational systems, they are not worthy of being saved by the entrepreneur. Therefore, it is clear that the education crisis cannot fix itself simply by breeding one or two lucky stars who flourish into successful businesspeople.

Fortunately, success is infectious, and it makes successful people seem like role models to young people, particularly those who yearn for success. Young people living in these minority communities can look up to other entrepreneurs like them as role models. It is vitally important for minority groups to witness successful people who look like them and who sound like them in order for those communities to discover the inspiration necessary to emulate those successful people. Individuals who have found success in business may utilize the resources that they have accumulated as a result of their accomplishments to help those in their communities who are struggling and give back to the community overall. They are able to start a cycle of inspiration that leads to success and then inspires them again, which may excite the minds of individuals in their community who only needed a little bit more motivation to succeed.

The tragic result of the actions of unscrupulous school

administrators and government officials has been that our children have been led astray as these actors cultivated a culture in which children are given the impression that nobody cares for them and nobody is rooting for their success. They do not have somebody to guide or serve as a model for them, therefore they do not have anyone who can encourage them to continue their education, improve their business acumen, or raise their general intelligence level. The terrible fact is that these children, rather than being encouraged at school, are treated as though they are criminals.

This cycle of poverty that befalls them, the lack of role models, and their subsequent pressure into joining gangs makes them wary of authority. This is the same authority that frequently forces them to pass through metal detectors prior to entering school, treating these children as criminals before they have even done anything wrong. Children's behavior is linked to how they are treated, and if society treats them like criminals, it engrains a mindset of self-doubt about their full capabilities.

When property prices are low, accessible funding is also limited. The low levels of financing that these schools in low-income neighborhoods obtain contribute to the low expectations that their students have for themselves, students are expected to develop the skills necessary to become self-starters, yet they seldom find anything to inspire them to light the spark that ignites the flame. Low expectations lead to low outcomes, very rarely will your expectations be exceeded. Zip codes should not dictate the level of resources, support, and education a child receives, yet that is the standard all across the United States, and this crisis has led to catastrophic failures throughout our education system.

This is due to the fact that schools utilize old, outdated textbooks; the facilities are in a constant state of disrepair; and teachers who are overworked and underpaid are forced to struggle with children who are not motivated, and they are forced to work in environments that are hazardous. It is no wonder that so many students fall victim to complacency because complacency has been an element of their entire lives. Complacency has followed them throughout their time in school as they were forced to deal with the worst systems imaginable. Complacency is thus learned, not innate. These students are effectively indoctrinated to accept their circumstances as they are and to accept the fact that their present conditions will remain for the remainder of their lives.

There is an old cliché that comes to mind about entrepreneurs that characterize them as uneducated and unsuccessful "C" students, despite them always being the most successful. This expression originates from the belief that successful businesspeople may achieve their goals without attending college or paying attention in class because they have discovered other, more time- and resource-efficient methods of success. In fact, the opposite is almost always true. Intelligent individuals are almost always successful businesspeople.

Their intelligence may have been innate or it may have been acquired through experience, but either way, they are always intelligent.

Most people will always conduct business with someone who has a college education, or those with a healthy moral frameworks, and the ability to think critically and solve problems as they arise. Bill Gates dropped out of Harvard, but he clearly was intelligent enough to obtain acceptance into Harvard in the first place. Being college educated may not be the best path for some, and acknowledging that does not mean we should not instill the importance of knowledge and education in our kids. In fact, it is an absolute necessity, particularly in today's competitive world.

If someone has been successful in turning a hobby or pastime into a lucrative business, they may not have to attend college if they have the appropriate drive and ability to think critically. However, to succeed, which, like anything else, is a process that takes time and work, does not happen overnight. Other communities have access to a diverse group of accomplished individuals who span industries, unlike many Black youth whose predominant models of success are athletes and entertainers. While we applaud their accomplishments, very few will ever make it in those industries.

But let us be absolutely certain about one thing: Business is not a conventional route at all. There are no guarantees in entrepreneurship; it is extremely risky. For this reason, having a foundational education is vital so that people may develop their own route and find success wherever they can make it. The road that each individual follows varies, and they each need a unique set of actions to reach their goals. Contrary to what is often learned in a regular educational setting, there is no one-size-fits-all approach to entrepreneurship. There is neither a set formula nor a standard procedure that one must adhere to in order to launch a business that is successful. Instead, the education that each and every one of us receives in the schools and communities where we live is very important to the process of determining what it is that will make us successful individuals in both business and in life.

The spirit of entrepreneurship is not shared by everybody. It is generally a perilous endeavor. It requires putting one's financial stability at risk, working long hours with no assurance of compensation, and taking up an endeavor that has a high probability of failure. After all, if everyone were an entrepreneur, there would be no need for entrepreneurs. Yet, this is the area where even more opportunities may be found: the opportunities that entrepreneurs create. Entrepreneurs in communities that do not have a significant amount of money may help their neighbors by ensuring that their companies are successful and continue to grow. This can give their neighbors a leg up in the workforce and help them launch successful careers in their own neighborhoods, attracting outsiders to invest further in the people in those communities.

Work is required to improve public education. The opportunity to find both the promise of success and the promise of life, liberty, and happiness that this country provides each and every one of us must be present in every minority community, and we must work to ensure that it is.

I am aware of the fact that the vast majority of minority children are and will be enrolled in the public education system. Because of this, I am even more convinced that we need to work toward improving the public education system rather than simply shifting our focus to trade schools, charter schools, and other private schooling systems that are profit-driven and in which only a small percentage of minorities will enroll.

Even though they have fallen so far behind, we must not give up on the public education system. Should we choose to act in this manner, we will be abandoning a whole generation. Instead, we should be fighting to ensure accountability and transparency in our public schools.

On the other hand, private schools are not held to the same standards of accountability as public schools, so they have an incentive to take shortcuts and fabricate an appearance of success where none exists. This is the reason why private schools are not the solution, nor are they the sole avenue for developing the entrepreneurial spirit in minority communities and for breaking the cycle of poverty that continues to exist within such communities.

Children's naturally inquisitive minds may be encouraged by the public school system just as effectively as they can be discouraged by it. To guarantee that our children are supplied with the means to discover success and generate wealth and opportunity for their communities, the people must collaborate with the government rather than the government working alone to achieve this goal. The alternative is for the government to work alone—an alternative that we cannot bear to risk.

It is easier to build up children than to repair broken men. This philosophy helps make sense of the challenges we face in the field of education. We will be condemned and will be confronted with the onerous task of correcting the broken who were failed by the school system if we do not work together to guarantee that students have the resources and power they need to achieve.

We will be able to witness the advantages of entrepreneurship and see how entrepreneurs can give back to the communities that raised them so long as we invest our time and efforts into improving our school systems.

2015: Carson at the Yad Vashem Holocaust Museum in Jerusalem for a moment of prayer.

2018: Carson as the keynote speaker at the Liberty University College of Osteopathic Medicine graduation.

ESSAYS BY
DR. BENJAMIN CARSON

THE CRISIS OF HEALTH CARE

It has often been stated that a good education is one of the best tickets to successfully achieving the American dream. Certainly, the ability to comprehend written documents and instructions, along with the ability to solve problems dealing with numerical elements, as well as having a basic knowledge of history can make navigating society much easier. The founders of this nation said that our system of governance is designed for an educated and informed populace. Of course, all of that makes a great deal of sense if you have a society where people are responsible for themselves and make their own decisions about the direction of their lives. It is not essential in a society where a monarch or ruling body makes decisions about what direction your life should take. Since we still live in a free society, we do a great disservice to anyone who is denied the opportunity to obtain a solid educational background. I think it would be reasonable to go a step further and say that denying a good education to any of our citizens is injurious to our society as a whole.

It is not uncommon for uneducated people to be under-achievers who have to be supported by other members of the community. It is also frequently the case that undereducated people feel disenfranchised and resentful of other more successful individuals because they feel that those individuals perhaps had an advantage which led to their success. The cultivation of these kinds of attitudes and beliefs, not unexpectedly, can lead to a mindset that justifies criminal activity in order to achieve a sense of equity. In settings where large numbers of people harbor these attitudes, criminal activity, which is frequently violent, is prevalent and the law-abiding citizens are losing a degree of freedom secondary to fear. One can easily conclude from this discussion that the havoc and chaos currently plaguing our society have many of their roots in the dismal educational environment that has been allowed to fester in many communities throughout our nation.

Since we know that people are largely products of the environment in which they develop, we should do everything we can to understand that environment and improve it. In places that have a very high failure rate in terms of public education, the crisis should be recognized and treated as an emergency. In a recent news report out of Baltimore for example, Jack Pannell, the former operator of a charter school in Baltimore city, said during an interview, "We start our school year by asking our parents, 'what are the hopes and dreams you have for your sons?' And it's the most emotional moment. And the hopes and dreams sometimes for those parents were, 'I hope my son lives to be eighteen years old.' Imagine that." said Pannell. The story was broadcast by the local news media which was highlighting the fact that twenty-one school-age children had already been murdered in only the first eight months of this year. Not only would the parents be worried, but many of the students would likely be very concerned about their own safety, which would impact their ability to concentrate on their studies.

I vividly remember being shown a gun by one of the students at my high school in Detroit as a youngster, and I must say it was a bit unnerving even though he said he was my friend and would use it to protect me if necessary. Knowing that there are guns and knives and other dangerous weapons in the place where you are supposed to be receiving an education can be very distracting. Can you even imagine what these environments are like for those students who simply want to have a good education to prepare them for life rather than being worried about their life?

I have witnessed the proliferation of feelings of despair and hopelessness in poor communities across this nation. Hopelessness is particularly harmful to young people who should be pursuing their education. I sadly remember when I was a failing student in grade school, giving up and just assuming that I would never understand the material that was being presented. I subsequently failed to pay attention to my teachers, which only exacerbated my lack of progress.

Many students move on to the next step, which is dropping out of school altogether. When that happens, opportunities for trouble multiply greatly. As the old saying goes, "Idle hands are the devil's workshop."

These feelings of hopelessness and unfairness render people easy targets for radical movements with nefarious purposes who like to use angry citizens to advance their hidden causes. There are organizations that proclaim themselves to be righteously working for the good of "the people." Closer scrutiny, however, often reveals avarice and dishonesty, which leads to the enrichment of the leaders of these movements while they do absolutely nothing for the warm bodies being used to intimidate others into providing financial ransoms. Needless to say, these types of organizations spend little or no time trying to improve the educational environment of those they claim to be so concerned about. If those they purported to care for really matter to them, they would be concerned about the quality of life, which is enhanced considerably by the type of education that turns warm bodies into capable, valuable employees and employers.

Whether it's gangs or other questionable organizations, they serve as huge distractions from gaining a good education and they contribute to the flourishing of unhealthy learning environments for young people. But we can't just wish for these organizations to go away and leave our children alone. We must realize that young people are attracted to these kinds of organizations because there is a void in their lives. If we want to create a healthy developmental environment for them, we must fill that void. That void is frequently caused by a sense of abandonment by family. No one wants to feel alone, especially when they are trying to discover their own identity. Gangs and violence are much less common in areas where there are strong traditional families and communities. This is one of the reasons why the two-parent household structure is so often attacked by these organizations.

We must not be intimidated by those who engage in name-calling and other hateful tactics simply because someone advocates for a strong two-parent household. We must understand that children and especially teenagers are filled with curiosity and are constantly exploring the unknown and trying to discover where they fit in. They must be welcomed with open arms by loving parents and other supportive adults who want to provide them with acceptance, advice, and love. That will go a long way toward improving their academic performance, but there are a number of other factors that negatively impact the educational environment.

Before looking at some of the other negative factors, let us make it abundantly clear that not all predominantly Black neighborhoods suffer from poor education. In the early twentieth century, there were communities like Greenwood Oklahoma, also known as Black Wall Street, where education was highly regarded and widely distributed amongst all the people. As a result, Greenwood, which is a suburb of

Tulsa, became known because of the prosperity of its people. They had strong traditional families and believed in hard work. There was absolutely no reason for the kids to get into trouble, and there was no void to fill—I should also mention that the churches were full every weekend. Regardless of the ethnicity of the populace, hard work, strong family support, and a solid education lead to prosperity, period. This was true one hundred years ago, and it is still true today.

Unfortunately, the Greenwood community was destroyed in perhaps the worst race riot in American history after a white woman falsely accused a Black man from the Greenwood community of sexual assault. To their credit, the citizens of Greenwood did not allow themselves to become victims and restored the town to its previous glory within a period of four years. Greenwood is an excellent example of how to gain success even in a hostile environment and how to be resilient and reject victimhood. Teaching these kinds of lessons to our young people would have a far greater beneficial effect than concentrating on meaningless topics that can be learned and understood simply through the procurement of a basic education.

Another issue that can have a profound impact on educational achievement is general physical health. Traditionally, poor people in this country have not been recipients of the best health care. In some cases, it is the system that is uncaring and, in other cases, the people themselves simply do not seek health care until it is too late to effect a cure.

As a child, I did not realize that everyone else could see the blackboard. While in the fifth grade, all the students were required to have an eye exam and it was discovered that my vision was so poor that I could almost have been qualified as disabled. After receiving a pair of pink-framed glasses, I was astonished that I could not only see the blackboard but could see the television without sitting a foot away from it. I immediately advanced from an F student to a D student, much to my delight and to the delight of my homeroom teacher, who had low expectations for me since I was the only Black student in the class.

There is no question that the expectations of the teacher with respect to each student impacts the way that they treat those pupils, which in turn has a profound effect on student performance or lack thereof. That brings us to the role of educators in low-achieving schools. I believe that many people enter the teaching profession with noble aspirations, but become discouraged when the only thing they get for doing an outstanding job is more work to do. Teachers, like everyone else, respond to both positive and negative reinforcement. They quickly lose their drive for excellence when they are not rewarded, and they frequently are not backed up regarding disciplinary measures toward unruly students. Then they get involved with teacher union groups that clearly have agendas other than the best education for students. It's not a good situation for anyone, but the victims who suffer most are the students.

Some public school systems, such as the one in Baltimore city, have enormous budgets which can be used for salary augmentation, but at the same time, they have miserable graduation rates, standardized testing, and college attendance. In most cases, they are not required to answer for the distressing performance of the students. When there is no accountability, there generally are tragic results. Good teachers with good results should be publicly and generously rewarded. There is no reason that teachers should be treated any differently than anyone else who is a professional in our society. I have no doubt that I would have been less successful without the aid and care of several outstanding teachers.

Acquiring the glasses was the first step in my remarkable academic transition, but there are still many students today who do not regularly get checked in terms of their vision, hearing, or other conditions that might impact their ability to learn. We would be very wise as a society to make sure that these kinds of screenings are not neglected, because we do not want to sacrifice the great potential of so many students who fall by the wayside because their underlying medical problems were not detected. Teachers and school administrators should be made aware of the kinds of conditions that can affect a child's learning ability. Sometimes, for instance, a student may be suffering from petit mal seizures, which are mild electrical disturbances in the brain that may look like daydreaming but in fact are treatable conditions. Urinary frequency, excessive pain, and unusual fatigue are things that should also arouse the suspicions of parents and teachers when seen in children.

It should not be lost on anyone that in many African American communities there is a distinct distrust of our medical system. Most people are familiar with the Tuskegee experiment in which government-sponsored research was done into the natural history of syphilis by following the lives of Black men who were infected with the sexually transmitted disease without receiving treatment. In many cases, the follow-up extended for decades while the bodies of the subjects were being ravaged, and many cases of death occurred while there were treatments that were readily available. Although this occurred a few decades ago, the resentment and distrust are alive and well, particularly amongst older African Americans. This mistrust translates into a diminished desire for routine checkups and preventive maintenance much to the detriment of Black communities. Having said that, the medical community needs to understand the origin of the distrust and do everything possible to be transparent and honest with people. More attention also needs to be devoted to disparities in health care that lead to marked differences in life expectancy for Black Americans versus white Americans. Currently, the average life expectancy for whites is 78.9 years while the life expectancy for Blacks in America is 74.8 years. That's a four-year difference.

As a Black male, those numbers should worry me, but they do not because I have had access to the best medical care available and it makes a difference. Twenty years ago, I experienced some urinary urgency and was initially diagnosed as having prostatitis. Antibiotics did not help, and a prostate biopsy demonstrated high-grade prostate cancer. I was able to undergo a nerve-sparing prostatectomy by the surgeon who invented the operation, and I'm here to tell the story twenty years later. At the time of my surgery, the cancer was only 1 millimeter away from breaking through the capsule, which would have led to its spread and probably my early demise. Furthermore, in 2020, I had a severe case of COVID and was near death, but was able to be treated with a monoclonal antibody infusion which saved my life. You can see what a difference access to high-quality medical care makes in terms of longevity.

We clearly have work to do in this area, because the state of one's health has a tremendous impact on the readiness of students for their academic endeavors. Students that are not healthy physically are unlikely to devote maximum attention to educational pursuits. This is why we need to seriously consider revamping our health-care system in this nation.

What is needed for good health care? The answer is to create a structure that involves only the health-care provider and the patient. In practically every medical scenario insurance companies facilitate the relationship, and all of a sudden, that middleman becomes the principal entity, controlling both the health-care system and the patients while extracting most of the monetary resources from the system. It is not that we don't devote enough money to the health care of our citizens, rather the problem is that we don't spend the money in an efficient manner. The money is used to prop up the system and enrich the facilitators, and not enough of it is devoted to the care of the patients. Upwards of 20 percent of our gross domestic product is devoted to health care. The average amount spent per US citizen is $12,530 per year, according to CMS.gov, which is an official United States government website. Yet we still have massive disparities amongst different groups in our nation and unwarranted confusion and delays. But I don't want to just complain, I want to propose a solution.

If every citizen had a health savings account over which they or, in the case of minors or mentally incompetent individuals, their guardians had control, it would be possible to return the relationship to the patient and the health-care provider. This would help bring transparency and efficiency to the system. It would also make both patients and health-care providers much more cognizant of the cost of various procedures and tests, which would automatically translate into more sensible expenditures of the allocated dollars. If family members could transfer dollars between accounts, each family would become a mini-insurance company. For example, if John Doe needed a procedure, and his health savings account was $500 short, his wife, his son, or his niece could transfer the money from their health savings account. Not only would this be extremely efficient, but it would cause families to work diligently to maintain every-one's health. If Uncle Johnny was smoking two packs of cig-arettes a day, everyone would be hiding his cigarettes and encouraging him to stop.

Also, in this system, the money would just continue to accumulate if you had good health and didn't need a lot of procedures or tests. At the time of one's death, the money in the health savings account could be passed on to a relative. In the case of many poor citizens who have never owned anything, this would be an opportunity to learn how to manage resources. Catastrophic health-care coverage would be managed by a separate policy, which would be much less expensive than private health-care policies, generally, because only catastrophic events would need to be covered. Obviously, there are many more details to such a program, but you can see how it is possible to simplify things and at the same time provide more efficient care. This accessibility to good care will clearly make a difference in the ability of students to concentrate on their studies.

Just how much does the government care about the edu-cation of disadvantaged students in our society? The COVID epidemic might shed some light on the subject. Largely at the behest of government-sponsored medical experts, schools were shut down for months and even years in some cases to avoid the possible spread of the coronavirus. The phrase "follow the science" was ubiquitous as a justification for shut-tering the educational facilities and thus the opportunities for advancement for many in our society. It was theorized that virtual learning from home with computers would be able to maintain academic progress amongst the students. As study after study demonstrated that students were rapidly losing ground academically, medical bureaucrats simply doubled down on their recommendations and let the educational carnage continue.

In poor communities, many students did not have access to high-speed internet, which made virtual learning extremely difficult. In so many cases, the students were already underachieving, and this additional blow put them on a trajectory of academic failure. The real tragedy is that so-called scientists were not following the science, which clearly demonstrated that school-age youngsters had very little chance of death or serious complications from the coronavirus. The scientific method in medicine requires that practitioners engage in a benefit-to-risk analysis before making recommendations. If that had been done, it would have become clear that the long-term damage from inferior educational endeavors was much greater than the damage caused by the virus. More vigorous effort should have been made to keep schools open, and at the same time, keep students safe. Hopefully, these lessons have been learned and will be applied in the future.

Seeing the results of this kind of decision-making along with the ever-changing recommendations for dealing with the coronavirus did nothing to improve trust in government-sponsored medical recommendations in not only the Black community but across the nation. I believe it would be very helpful for governmental bureaucrats to admit that they made bad decisions that negatively impacted the citizens of our nation and that they will be more transparent and will truly follow the science in the future. Of course, they must follow through with those promises and not just utter empty words. What a wonderful example it would be to students if these powerful people could exhibit a bit of humility.

As you can see, there is a plethora of factors that impact the educational environment for our young people. One that we have not discussed yet is motivation. I was motivated to become a doctor by listening to stories about missionary doctors in church. Sometimes when the going got rough and I wanted to give up, I was motivated by a desire to escape poverty. Different motivations work for different people, but almost everyone would like to be rich. It is very unfortunate that the media portrays sports and entertainment as the way to get rich quickly. So many youngsters that come from impoverished backgrounds are seduced by the constant idolization of sports and movie stars, and they devote their energies to achieving stardom as a rapper, quarterback, or superhero. Of course, the likelihood of their achieving success as a professional sports star or entertainer is extremely small. When the 99-plus percent of those young people realize that their hopes and dreams are going to be disappointed, many of them have already put academic pursuits on the back burner and are left struggling with decisions about their future.

I have nothing against sports and entertainment stars, and I congratulate those who achieve success in those areas, but I would encourage them to give the young people who are trying to emulate them the truth about how limited that pathway to success is. Instead, encourage them to pursue academic excellence while working hard to achieve their dream of stardom. If that dream fails, as is highly likely, they will still have a path to success. Some of those young people would also benefit by knowing that there are more than 1.5 million Black millionaires in the United States, the vast majority of whom are not sports stars or entertainers. Most are entrepreneurs and professionals who understand the value of education and hard work. They have also chosen to pursue pathways that are more likely to yield success based on their hard work and dedication as opposed to fields that require a degree of good fortune along with the hard work to succeed. There are many people with heavenly voices who will never achieve stardom because they were not at the right place at the right time with the right people hearing them. There are many young men with incredible basketball skills who will never come close to being an NBA player, not because they're not good enough, but simply because they were not discovered by the right people. Those are things that are not under their control, and therefore, it is wise not to put all of one's eggs in a basket that they can't control.

I visit many schools around the country on a regular basis and talk to the young people about the tremendous potential that resides in each one of them and about the almost limitless opportunities that exist in our society regardless of one's ethnicity. The young people are very responsive, and I believe it would be extremely advantageous for school systems around the country to engage inspirational speakers who can provide tremendous motivation and examples with which the young people can identify.

My mother grew up in an impoverished environment in rural Tennessee and never had a chance to advance beyond the third grade. However, she is the wisest person I ever knew. That wisdom led her to fight vigorously for the proper education of her two sons. I remember her fighting school administrators who wanted my brother to be in a vocational curriculum, and my mother insisted that he be in the college preparatory curriculum. She won and so did my brother, who became a rocket scientist. It should not be necessary for parents to go through those kinds of battles in order to obtain a valuable education for their children. We as a society must recognize the great potential we are losing when we don't do everything possible to empower the next generations with an outstanding education. Well-educated people are very difficult to manipulate and deceive. Those who wish to fundamentally change America away from a nation that is of, by, and for the people, to a nation that is of, by, and for the government are not necessarily desirous of a well-informed populace, and thus, they are very tolerant of a dysfunctional educational system that deprives young people of proper motivation and knowledge. If this educational dysfunction in our public school systems is to be rectified, it is going to require courage, knowledge, and unremitting dedication on behalf of we the people.

THE CRISIS OF FAITH

Faith was very important to the founders of our nation. Our Declaration of Independence specifically states that our rights come from God and not from government. Our founders did not always act in a Christlike manner, and they had a strong sense of rationalization that allowed them to brutalize the Native American population and engage in the horrific slave trade. Nevertheless, the Bible was used in the one-room schoolhouses, and the difference between right and wrong was strongly emphasized. John Adams, our second president. even said that our Constitution was designed for a moral and religious people and was wholly inadequate for the governance of any other.

Many of the European settlers managed to convince themselves that the Black slaves did not have souls and were more closely related to animals than to themselves. It became progressively more difficult for them to hold these kinds of opinions after the slaves learned to speak English and were able to express themselves—quite eloquently in some cases. Eventually, it was the abolitionists, who were strongly motivated by spirituality, that played a magnificent role in ridding our nation of the scourge of slavery.

Many Marxist writers have commented on the fact that America is very strong because of our families and our faith. These comments were made because they felt that the only way to bring America down was to destroy those two entities. One does not have to be very observant to see that our faith and our families have been and continue to be under extreme attack. As we begin to replace faith in God with faith in government, the whole nature of our nation is changing, and not for the better. History teaches us that Marxist/Leninist regimes are anxious to do away with any aspect of the civilization they are conquering that inspires the people and makes them less docile. They also are anxious to distort or destroy the history of such civilizations because they realize that the history provides the identity of the populace, and identity is that thing on which the beliefs are based. American society today is faced with the challenge of those who are attempting to distort our history and replace it with myths that are more consistent with the ideology that drives them.

If we want to preserve freedom in America and the tremendous opportunities that have attracted so many to our shores, our schools must once again educate the students about world history, including Marxism and the litany of similar ideologies, their tactics of historical distortion, and how they have destroyed societies. If they don't know what has happened in the past, they will not be able to recognize the forces that are attempting to manipulate them and change our country. I cannot emphasize strongly enough the incredibly important role played by educators in our schools in maintaining the accuracy of the history they teach. When teaching American history, they must expose the students to the good, the bad, and the ugly, but the real lessons are derived from where the emphasis is placed. Those who just emphasize the bad and the ugly create a sense of resentment and shame while those who accurately tell both sides of the story will see that there is a lot more good than there is bad and ugly.

Teaching our children that America is uniquely evil because slavery existed here is less than honest. Yes, we had slavery and that must be acknowledged and discussed at length, but so did virtually every society depicted in written history. What is unique about the United States is the fact that we had so many people who adamantly opposed the practice of slavery that we fought a bloody Civil War, losing a large portion of our population in order to abolish it. Many students today are also taught that America is systemically racist and that white people are oppressors, while Black people and other minorities are victims. Obviously, if America was such an evil, racist place, people immigrating here would dissuade their families from coming; but, they do not because they know the opportunity they, as minorities, have here, which is not impeded by racism. Considering the rise in immigration into the United States, this clearly is not happening, which tells you all you need to know about the lack of veracity in this kind of education. Our society is plagued by powerful individuals who say to the people, "Don't believe your eyes, your ears, or your heart. Just believe what we tell you and be happy." People who are not well informed, and a lot of our young people who are not sophisticated, are vulnerable to this kind of propaganda. This is why education was emphasized so strongly in the early centuries of this country, and this is why we must rapidly return to a place where we recognize that our entire system is dependent upon well-informed and educated people.

Recent national polling indicates that only two-thirds of Americans now consider themselves religious or as having a relationship with God. Prayer and associated studies were essentially banned from the public education arena in the early 1960s. Many schools used to post the Ten Commandments prior to that time. Now that would be anathema to the minority of persons who reject religion and the moral guideposts it provides. Yet the situation begs the question; what's wrong with saying "thou shall not kill, thou shall not steal, thou shalt not bear false witness, thou shalt not envy, thou shall not commit adultery, and honor your parents," among other things? When you combine withholding the teaching of morality with abundant exposure to every kind of vice imaginable, is it any wonder that crime, violence, and hatred are running rampant and escalating in America today?

One of the enduring strengths of America is our emphasis on family structure. The family was the place where our young people received their moral compass. It was the place where they found comfort and they were valued by their families, reducing the need for external approval. Attempting to satisfy those external needs for approval often leads to a significant compromise of one's value system. With the breakdown of traditional family structure, particularly in the Black community, combined with the emergence of educators who feel obligated to convert students to their ideological thinking, indoctrination is alive and well in our public school systems. All of this has been exposed to the public recently, and we need to decide whether we are going to tolerate it or insist that teachers and schools concentrate on making sure that students develop facility with our language, mathematical skills, understanding of scientific principles, understanding of how the government works, and learning world as well as American history.

There are many more useful things that can be taught to our children without engaging in political indoctrination and manipulation. As Abraham Lincoln said, "a house divided against itself cannot stand." That means we should be teaching our students that we the American people are not each other's enemies, even if we have disagreements. The reason we have brains and the ability to express ourselves is so that we can work out those disagreements and coexist harmoniously. The "my way or the highway" philosophy leads to a bunch of aimlessly wandering vagrants, or to a docile, dominated population. Neither of those options is acceptable for the United States of America.

Teaching members of racial minorities that they are hopelessly handicapped in a systemically racist society certainly does not encourage their vigorous pursuit of an education in such a system. What it does encourage is the development of radical ideas about how to oppose such a system, and these young people become easy fodder for those wishing to fundamentally change America. If a person thinks that they are a victim, they will begin to act like a victim and think like a victim and, ultimately, they are victims. Their entire demeanor, physical, mental, and spiritual becomes that of a victim. Instead, we should be making every effort to empower all students by emphasizing the potential that exists in each of them.

In virtually every city and community there are powerful stories of people who have overcome poverty and hardship to become highly successful. There are few such individuals who would not welcome an opportunity to share their path to success with our students. Instead of constantly emphasizing negativity, emphasizing opportunity and accomplishment will have a powerful healing effect on those children who are struggling with their self-image.

To emphasize what a powerful impact the mind and mental state have on the body, think about what would happen if you were in a room with a small group of people and a hungry tiger walked into the room. Your heart rate would increase tremendously as would your blood pressure, and there would be changes in your bladder sphincter and in your respiratory rate as your body prepared for the fight or flight mode without the tiger ever laying a paw on you. Now think about what would happen to you if you were in a constant atmosphere of stress. The physical, mental, and spiritual toll would be ongoing and extremely deleterious.

In healthy settings where a student has a caring family and a healthy educational environment, a great amount of attention is devoted to the psychological well-being of the student. In situations where students come from dysfunctional home settings and then attend schools where they feel neither cared for nor relevant, the likelihood of them exerting the necessary energy to excel academically is extremely small. Some will say I'm painting a hopeless picture for so many students, but that is not true. I simply realize that we must know what we're up against in order to be victorious in the long run. No one has all the answers, but if we can agree on the nature of the problem, I think we have the intellectual capacity by working together to solve it. Having said that, victimhood and hopelessness are very difficult problems to eliminate.

After repeated failures to improve oneself, there is a natural tendency to give up and accept defeat. That's where faith comes in. The Bible talks about how many times God is willing to forgive us for the same mistake. It makes the point that God's forgiveness is limitless because he loves us. Faith helps us to trust in a power that is greater than ourselves, and in a power that loves us and wants the best for us. Yet, ideologies like Marxism, on the other hand, expend much effort in trying to convince people that their horrible circumstances are controlled by someone else, and that they are hopeless victims unless they place their faith in the designated leaders. For America, replacing faith in God with faith in government is one of their ultimate goals.

None of that type of propaganda used to go on in our schools when we readily acknowledged our Judeo-Christian foundation and were taught to love our neighbors as ourselves. Power-hungry individuals absolutely abhor any mention of religion, because religion releases people from the stranglehold of victimhood. Yet how ridiculous is it that we forbid teaching about God while at the same time acknowledging through our founding document, the Declaration of Independence, that our rights come from God? How do we logically forbid public discussions about God in our schools, but allow items to be purchased with our money on which are printed the words "in God we trust." Obviously, there is a bit of hypocrisy involved here. Those who want to conquer America by destroying our faith and our families have made great strides in recent decades, but they have not completely won yet. Their ability to complete their victory will depend on whether we reject our history and our identity or embrace who we are and what made us the greatest nation in the history of the world.

As mentioned earlier, the attitude and approach that teachers take toward their teaching assignments have a tremendous impact on the enthusiasm, or lack thereof, of the students. We all remember those teachers who were full of wonderful stories and illustrations and brought the lessons to life with interesting props versus the teachers who boringly sat at their desks and had you read during class time. In my experience, the interesting teachers seldom had to deal with disruptive students, because such students interrupted the good time other students were having, which made them quite unpopular. Also, the teachers who made an effort to get to know each student were generally rewarded with more cooperation and effort. Principals and administrators should engage with the stellar teachers and provide mechanisms for them to share successful techniques with new teachers or those having great difficulty teaching students.

A hands-on approach to teaching students to respect each other even when different opinions are voiced is critically important going forward. When students go home and turn on the television, they frequently see voices of hatred and division; it would be wonderful if they could consistently find voices of compassion and unity in the classroom.

Encouraging students to vigorously advance their own ideas at the expense of others and to seek refuge when their feelings are hurt is ultimately of no value to the student or to the society to which they belong. Encouraging open discussion of varying opinions, on the other hand, stimulates creative thinking and discussions that contribute to an understanding and compassionate attitude. As frequently is the case, when the discussion leads to the topic of faith, that discussion should not be suppressed. If some people complain that there is an attempt to force morality on them, it should be observed that perhaps others feel that immorality is being forced on them and that open discussions that explore the basis of belief systems can be helpful to everyone.

Sometimes you have very good teachers who still face very disruptive students, and they have a very difficult time presenting the materials they have prepared for class. These teachers should make it clear to students who want to learn that they would be willing to talk with them after class or after school at an appointed time. As a student of an inner-city high school in Detroit, I frequently found myself going back after school to talk to the teachers and asking them what they were intending to teach. The vast majority of them were absolutely delighted to share the information with me and to provide extra tutelage. Any time you can get a student in a poor educational environment to recognize that they must be responsible for their own education, you can set ablaze a flame of thirst for knowledge that will not be extinguished and will seek its own way of obtaining knowledge. I hasten to add that the race of the teacher didn't make any difference. They were all anxious to share their knowledge with me.

If we really want minority students in poor educational environments to excel, we would do well to de-emphasize the significance of ethnic differences. That does not mean that we shouldn't be proud of our ancestors, but it does mean that constantly harping on race and making accusations of racism is unlikely to contribute to an atmosphere of academic success. In a multiethnic society, peaceful coexistence is more likely to be achieved by concentrating on our common aspirations and dreams than by concentrating on divisive issues. We must teach our students that it is their brain and their character that define who they are, and not their skin color, the texture of their hair, or the shape of their noses. Those latter things are external physical characteristics that provide variety but do not define who a person is. Try to imagine how difficult it would be to concentrate on learning if you have been indoctrinated to believe that the teacher hates you and everyone who looks like you. This is not to say that racism doesn't exist, but it has been largely diminished in American society. We must not allow our young people to be poisoned into believing that racism exists around every corner and in every spoken communication. Those who wish to divide and conquer our society must not be allowed to succeed.

As long as there is evil in the world, there will be unfairness, but we don't have to be controlled by it. That is the beauty of what faith in God can do for us. It was that faith that allowed a ragtag army commanded by General George Washington to defeat the most powerful military empire on earth. It was that faith that empowered the Union Army to defeat the Confederate Army and the institution of slavery in America. It was that faith that provided the courage that powered the civil rights movement in America. It is that faith that can allow us to work together to create a functioning and efficient educational system for every child in America. Banning God and godlike principles from public schools is not something that is supported by the Constitution. God-inspired principles like loving your neighbor, caring for the helpless, developing your talents to the utmost so that you become valuable to the people around you, and having values and principles that govern your life can only improve society and certainly have done so in the past.

Imagine the following scenario:

A missionary discovers two starving children deep in the forest. They are near death, but fortunately the missionary has some very nutritious porridge and begins to feed them. They quickly gain strength, but one of the children decides that they don't like the porridge and that it should be done away with because it offends them. If that wish is granted, they both continue their path to starvation. If the porridge is made available and they are given a choice, only one of them will have to starve and the other can continue to gain strength and thrive. Perhaps the other would reconsider his choice as time goes on. Religion should not be forced on anyone, but the principles of love and acceptance and excellence as advocated via biblical principles certainly should not be avoided.

The bottom line is we get to decide how we want to raise our children. Do we want to teach them to love your neighbor or destroy your neighbor if they don't agree with you? Do we want to teach them the "can-do" attitude or the "what can you do for me" attitude? Do we want to teach them to respect the opinions of others, or do we want to teach them that their opinion is the only one that matters? Do we want to encourage them to do their best or to give up because the system is stacked against them? Do we want to teach them to do everything they can to uplift their community and their nation, or do we want to buy into the philosophy that we live in an evil nation, and it should be resisted? The choice is ours.

THE CRISIS OF PARTICIPATION

———

The difference a good education makes in a free society, such as the one that we have, cannot be overemphasized. Not only do well-educated people earn substantially more money, but they also tend to be exposed to greater opportunities and frequently are less prone to manipulation by dishonest people who are always on the prowl for victims. We often point a finger at middle school and high school when it comes to academic failures, but the fact is that failure frequently starts much sooner. It's good to remember that in grades one, two, and three we learn to read, but after that, we read to learn. Multiple studies have demonstrated that a child who is reading at grade level by grade three is much more likely to graduate from high school than one who has not attained that milestone. This means that we should pour a lot more effort into reading proficiency early on with virtually every student in our nation.

I was not a big fan of reading as a youngster until my mother forced me to read books and submit book reports to her, which she couldn't read, but we didn't know that. I quickly discovered that reading was actually more entertaining than watching television. One has to use one's own imagination to convert the words on the page into concepts, whereas someone has already used their imagination to produce television programs. And while they derive significant intellectual benefit from so doing, the viewers of that program generally receive significantly less benefit. Once I began to enjoy reading, the library became a vast, unexplored New World of excitement. I became a bookworm and greatly enjoyed becoming a source of knowledge for my classmates and others in my environment. To say that reading changed the trajectory of my life would be a huge understatement.

This is the reason that my wife, Candy, and I, through the Carson Scholars Fund, place reading rooms in schools throughout the nation. We primarily target Title I schools where libraries are poorly funded or nonexistent. These rooms are thematic and depict the areas in which they are located. For instance, there is one near a NASA launching location that is decorated like a space capsule. When you look through one window you see the moon, through another window you see the earth, and through yet another window you see E.T. They have hundreds of books, most of which are donated, that would capture the interest of almost any child. The children can gain rewards for reading books, but the biggest reward is an interest in learning and greatly improved academic performance.

Of course, there will be some who argue about the value of reading and advocate other mechanisms of learning, and you can find studies to support almost any position on the topic of education, but common sense should tell us that students who feel valued and supported do better in their academic pursuits and in life, generally speaking. Every attempt should be made early on to equip them with the tools that enhance their chances of success. One of those tools is the ability to analyze the validity of what they are reading. I believe schools would be wise to enlist the aid of many professionals who are quite adept at analyzing literature and studies. Many people in the scientific and medical community would be delighted to be guests at schools where they could teach children to evaluate data and evidence in a logical and proven way. I'm sure some of those students would then share that information with their parents, which would go a long way toward helping us to achieve a more informed and educated society, and that in turn would greatly strengthen our nation.

Physicians are people of significant academic achievement who are readily available. Some of the established practitioners of medicine would be happy to volunteer half a day a month to show students how the body works and many other aspects of basic science that when explained and illustrated in interesting ways would captivate the imaginations of students who otherwise would be disinterested in school. These scientifically inclined individuals have been trained for many years to use facts and evidence when making decisions.

It is quite possible that if physicians had been available to students nationwide during the coronavirus pandemic, a lot of vigorous conversations about natural immunity would have occurred, and those discussions would have overflowed from the classrooms into the streets, homes, and legislative offices—perhaps stimulating a more scientifically robust approach to the disease. Physicians might have been in a position where they did not have to feel intimidated into only providing opinions that were in sync with governmental talking points. The fact that so many highly trained individuals yielded to the threats and pressure to conform should make us all cognizant of the power of our government to curtail free speech and why such speech must be protected at all times and in all settings. Not only high schools, but colleges and universities must become sites of vigorous debate and the presentation of many views regarding solutions to problems in our society. As the Bible says, there is safety in the multitude of voices.

Mental health experts can be of particular value in school settings since they can help teachers learn to identify disturbing patterns of thinking, and in many cases intervene before those patterns of thinking erupt into violent, sometimes fatal, behavior. These professionals can also help identify and prevent the inculcation of political ideology into the curriculum. Our schools should be beacons of learning rather than institutions of political indoctrination. Obviously, medical professionals, just like teaching professionals, should be screened and monitored lest they become sources of further problems rather than solutions.

Young people today are exposed to all types of characters to emulate through electronic media. Many of those characters are unsavory, to say the least. At the same time, there are abundant, very positive role models readily available to schools across this nation. Giving children a chance to meet these individuals and ask them questions about their lives and their careers can be immensely beneficial. Children might not otherwise have an opportunity to meet a rocket scientist, an archaeologist, an architect, or an entrepreneurial inventor. When children begin to see people like this with very interesting lives who can give relevance to some of the materials that they are learning in school, their enthusiasm for learning is likely to increase significantly.

At the same time, it can be very useful to expose the students to people who have made significant mistakes in their lives, sometimes resulting in incarceration. Many such individuals have been rehabilitated or are on their way to reentering society and in some cases can be brought before students via live-video chat or video presentations. Such individuals can make a much greater impression on the students than someone they considered as "Mr. Goody Two-Shoes" trying to tell them about criminal activities and how to avoid getting involved in them.

As was mentioned earlier, many students are seduced by dreams of enormous wealth and stardom because of the emphasis on sports and entertainment in our society. It is good to teach that, in our society, when people need you because of the skills you possess, they will pay you well. That seems like a simple concept, but it doesn't hit home for many students until they're able to see it with their own eyes. There's absolutely nothing wrong with showing students salaries that can be expected with certain careers, but they should also be shown what can happen when the entrepreneurial spirit is admixed with skill.

Many large corporations were started by individuals with a certain skill set who parlayed that into a big business. I recently met a man in Texas who started out sweeping floors and ended up as the CEO of a large international business. My mother went out of her way to expose me to people of accomplishment, and I think it kindled a spark that could not be extinguished. For many students, the classroom would be the only mechanism for such exposure. It costs nothing and exposes students to potentially life-changing opportunities and ideas.

Classrooms should be places where interesting discussions take place and that stimulate students to want to further investigate the subject matter on their own. I certainly learned more outside the classroom than I did inside because I was stimulated to read. There is certainly nothing wrong with having students discuss controversial current events.

They should be encouraged to look at issues from multiple vantage points, and teachers should ask students to advocate for points of view that they don't necessarily agree with. This will help them to be more tolerant of other ideas. Obviously, it would be good to have these discussions available for parents to make sure that students were not being led into dangerous territory. These kinds of discussions prepare students to think for themselves and not just be sheeplike followers of whatever is being advocated by others.

One of the very large problems that has occurred particularly in public schools is social promotions—the practice of moving students on to the next grade even when they are not ready so as to promote greater self-esteem. Some teachers and administrators have been led to believe that it harms students to keep them back when they clearly are not ready to move on to the next level. I suspect that more harm is done by putting students in an academic situation where they are unlikely to be successful, which is even more injurious to their self-image. It should also be noted that many teachers organize their lesson plans in such a way that the least capable students can grasp the material. This is absolute torture for the more advanced students who sometimes then lose their enthusiasm for learning. They become bored and frequently become troublemakers. This is just one of the negative ramifications that can emanate from social promotions. In the ideal setting, one would not wait until the end of the semester to decide the fate of failing students. The earlier the intervention, the more likely academic success will be achieved, but if it is not achieved, another semester or two in a less stressful educational environment might allow slower students to catch up.

Social promotions should be absolutely forbidden. They negate the whole purpose of schools and they teach students to feel entitled instead of teaching them that advancement can be earned by merit. Social promotion is tantamount to a dereliction of duty. Severe penalties should be imposed on those involved in this nefarious practice. It calls into question whether those teachers and administrators really care about the students and their chances of living a successful life and achieving the American dream.

It is difficult to find a successful person who cannot point to a teacher who played a significant role in their success. I certainly remember many who worked very hard to put me on the right pathway and keep me on that pathway to success. But it would be quite naïve to assume that all students have good teachers. By the same token, some teachers with very good intentions and skills are precluded from using these by various curriculum requirements imposed by school boards and administrators. It is also true that close to 50 percent of teachers quit within the first five years, meaning that a large number of teachers are quite inexperienced. If we want quality teaching, we must pay much closer attention to the training and remuneration of those we put in charge of teaching our children. We also need to provide some protection for teachers who don't want to join the teacher unions or might want to have an alternative union that is focused on the children.

When it comes to teaching science and math, there is a significant shortage of competent teachers and very often those classes are taught by people who did not major or even minor in STEM areas. This undoubtedly has something to do with our poor showing on international science and math-related testing. It's difficult for schools to compete for these individuals because they can earn very substantial salaries elsewhere. This is why I suggested earlier inviting scientists, physicians, and others into the classroom as guest presenters—certainly until such time as we are willing to do what is necessary to attract teachers with the requisite knowledge and skills to develop student competency and interest in STEM-related areas.

Perhaps the area that requires the most attention in terms of effecting a real change in the educational quality of our children is the political arena. Many politicians in the areas where schools are failing make big promises but are very inconsistent in terms of their delivery. It is up to the voters to demand from them an accounting of where the dollars are spent that fattened the coffers in the Department of Education. What results are we getting for the vast amount of dollars we spend on each child? I remember some years ago during the "no child left behind" era, several Baltimore public schools failed the children, and arrangements were being made to transfer those children to schools with passing marks. Several of the local politicians blocked the effort to transfer those students. Were they really doing those students a favor?

Unless these politicians are held responsible for educational failures in their districts, it is highly unlikely that they will be motivated to put forth the effort necessary to alter these dismal scenarios. Voters should scrutinize the efforts of the entire political spectrum from the governor to the school board. An active group of parents advocating for educational excellence will quickly gain the trust of neighborhoods and can be a powerful force to rectify the ills that are producing unprepared students.

Perhaps even more effective than voting nonproductive politicians out of office is running for office yourself. We live in a democratic republic, which means that we the people elect from amongst ourselves people who will represent our interests. All it takes is one dedicated parent on the school board to thwart blatantly political agendas that are being forced down the throats of teachers, and subsequently, students. Groups of parents in economically deprived areas can also begin to agitate for a different mechanism for funding their schools. A common mechanism is through millage taxes, which basically means that a lot of school-dedicated tax money is derived from such taxes in affluent neighborhoods, and very little money allotted for schools is derived from poor neighborhoods where incomes are limited. This kind of system creates permanent inequality of educational resources and makes it much more difficult for children in poor neighborhoods to achieve educational success.

It benefits our entire society if we find ways to equalize educational resources and subsequently opportunities for the poor. One resource that is desperately needed in poor neighborhoods is high-speed internet. It is very frustrating trying to do homework with spotty internet coverage. Education must be a priority for authorities to install the requisite infrastructure for this necessity. Until that permanent infrastructure is in place, it is possible to bring in trucks with portable cell towers that can cover a substantial geographical area. I learned about this while serving as the Secretary of the United States Department of Housing and Urban Development. Again, it is a matter of where the priorities of those making decisions reside.

Future advances in technology, if used appropriately, can significantly ameliorate educational inequalities to offset a dearth of other resources. Three-dimensional virtual reality headsets are becoming commonplace and much more realistic. Soon it will be possible to truly attend a virtual classroom and be exposed to the very best teachers in the United States and indeed in the world. It will be possible to actually visit the Roman empire or have a ringside seat during the Peloponnesian wars. Poor students will have the same kind of advantages in learning as students from wealthy families if we decide to distribute these resources equitably. But we must also remember how difficult it is to get many young people away from video games now. Can you imagine how much more difficult it will be to control their activities when they can disappear into a virtual world of their own creation? It means that with every advance in educational techniques we must be aware of the downside ramifications and proactively manage them.

I hope this book demonstrates the need for us to consider the failure of the educational system in several parts of our country a national emergency, which requires nonpartisan solutions, not today, but yesterday. It will be impossible to maintain an equitable democratic republic if we do not have an informed and educated populace. It is time to recognize that we the American people are not each other's enemies, but ignorance among the people is everyone's enemy. If we work together and acknowledge the existence of the problem, we will be victorious and, more importantly, our students will be the recipients of the freedom and prosperity derived from a good education.